COPEN HAGEN FOOD

TRINE HAHNEMANN

COPEN HAGEN FOOD

TRINE HAHNEMANN

Stories, traditions and recipes

Photography by Columbus Leth

quadrille

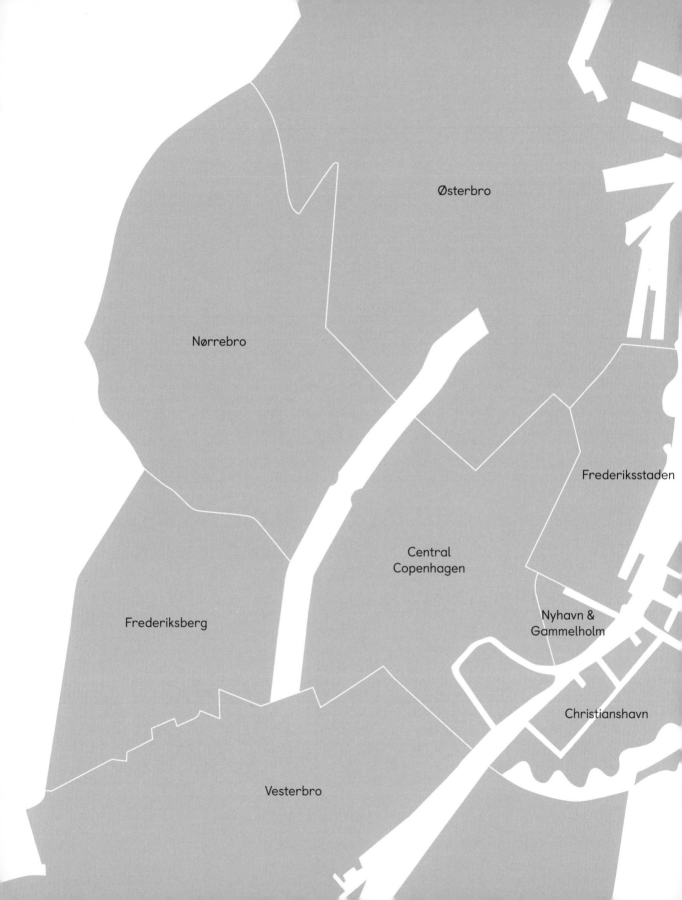

This painting by Vilhelm Hammershøi symbolizes for me living in Copenhagen: the apartments with rooms en suite, the emptiness and the colours, the Nordic cool. Hammershøi painted this apartment again and again. The picture seems calm, content and lonely, and timeless. It is a painting of everyday life which Hammershøi inhabits with nearly nothing, so I look for stories. I always feel drawn to his paintings. I like to just sit on a chair and observe quietly with my hands folded in my lap. Even though this was painted more than 100 years ago, there is something profound going on for me – a sense of belonging. I can imagine myself as a child sitting on the chair listening to the silence while I swing my legs in my own rhythm, waiting for something to happen.

In this book I have described my home town, Copenhagen. It is not a general guide book; it's my history of my city. This is the way I live in Copenhagen. I am not a young hipster; I have not just moved here. I was born and bred here and most of my history was made in this town. So, it is a very personal book about the place I grew up in and still live in.

While I have been getting on with my life, Copenhagen has become a cosmopolitan city, a place famous for its restaurants, coffee, bicycling culture, friendliness and *hygge*. Whole neighbourhoods have gone through major transformations for both good and bad. The restaurant scene has evolved tremendously; we now have great wine bars and cocktail bars, food from around the world, street food markets.

I have not mentioned all the places that deserve attention; there are a lot of wonderful spots not necessarily on my radar. New things happen all the time. I have aimed to capture the atmosphere and relate it to the history that I know. It is far from the full picture. This is my Copenhagen.

Since I do live here, I have routines more than adventures, things that I do without

thinking. I think the moments when I am conscious about what it means for me to live here, is when I return from my travels. There are a few things that I will have missed, not least my morning walks – and I have several routes here.

I walk around the six lakes that define the city's boroughs. Or I walk down to the waterfront, over the pedestrian bridge at Østbanegade down to The Little Mermaid, then along the water until I reach Nyhavn. There, I will cross the bridge over the harbour to Christianshavn to have a coffee, and then I will go back home over Kongens Nytorv, down through Gothersgade, then cross the King's Garden to get home.

Or, I will bicycle from my house at Østerbro to the waterfront, along the water to Nyhavn, over the bridge at Nyhavn, go down Strandgade, turn right toward the water after Knippelsbro, continue along the water and over Cirkelbroen – the Olafur Eliasson bridge – and continue to Islands Brygge along the water until I reach the next pedestrian bridge, keep going to Sønder Boulevard and along there to my friend Keld's place, Kihoskh (pictured on the front cover of this book). I'll stop there for coffee and a sandwich, then bicycle to Værnedamsvej and stop to look at books at Thiemers Magasin, then continue along the lakes all the way home, which means that I will bicycle through three boroughs and Frederiksberg. Sometimes I take a detour down to Sankt Hans Torv to have coffee either at Kaffeplantagen or Mirabelle.

The other thing that is equally important to me is to drive out to the woods at Dyrehaven for a walk. That goes for all the seasons. In just 20 minutes you are out of town with more space, lovely views and ancient trees, and a special kind of calm. I believe that what makes a place home is to repeat habits and enjoy the reunion after a spell away. Copenhagen is my home for better and for worse.

Opposite: Vilhelm Hammershøi, *De fire stuer*, 1914

I came into this world at the hospital that I can see every day from the end of my street, though I now look at it from the other side of the Copenhagen lakes. I grew up in a street near to where I live today. But, while I have lived most of my life in Copenhagen, I have also raised a family in America and the UK, and spent a lot of time daydreaming about all the other places I could live, though I've always found myself returning 'home' again. In other words, I have spent my life trying to understand what it means to belong in a place, how a city's identity influences you, and this book is – in part – my attempt to hammer that out, while exploring with you the truly magnificent city of my birth.

Cities are spaces organically carved out and defined by their changes over time, yet history leaves its trails and stories through each city's architecture, people, markets… and not least through the ways in which it feeds itself. Each city in the world is unique, with its own tempo, smells, noises and characters.

When you have lived in the centre of a city on and off for nearly 50 years, as I have, the space and the buildings change and the people move around; some move in, others move out. But the city remains, with its soul and identity intact.

When I was little, my dream was to escape to New York as soon as I had grown up, and so I did. I felt at home right away, in a new and different way than I did in Copenhagen. Maybe it's because I never chose Copenhagen. When I grew up here, it was a provincial town, even boring in many ways, with not a lot going on. The other people around were mostly native Danes. If you heard another language spoken, you would spin your head round to look at these new people… you almost wanted to ask for their autograph! Back then, I longed for something bigger. These days all such thoughts are banished: in just a few brief years, Copenhagen has become an exciting, dynamic and cosmopolitan city with a new jewel to discover around nearly every corner. Now the world flocks here.

I have always lived in cities and I used to think I would die if I was forced to live in the countryside. That has changed. I have grown to love the country, its silence, the different pace, the unruliness of nature, the changing seasons and most of all the sense that nature is bigger than you. This development has come about through my relationship with food. I have discovered a deep understanding and appreciation of the countryside and the people who live and work there. They grow the food and thus allow cities to work; in return, the countryside feeds the cities I love so much.

As a child I spent a lot of time imagining that I was a member of another family. Actually, I had several lives in several different families. I loved sitting in the dark on my windowsill, looking into the other apartments and wishing that I lived there. In my mind, I decorated the rooms and made up stories about the other family members, what they did, the conversations we would have, what we would eat, the cakes I would bake…

Life can carry us in various ways and we get inspired by these whimsical imaginings as well as – more tangibly – by chance encounters, and we learn new things from each opportunity that comes our way. We make choices, both good and bad, but I do believe that living in a city makes our possibilities more diverse; there is simply a bigger chance for things to happen, as we will meet far more people along the way.

Then there are all the people you didn't meet and all the choices you didn't make. That is where storytelling begins. I still tell stories to myself when I am walking around Copenhagen. I can't help myself; they just come to me on morning walks around the city, looking at all the things that go on.

This is a truly inspiring city, a place that feeds romantic storytelling souls and rewards exploration many hundreds of times over. Welcome to my Copenhagen.

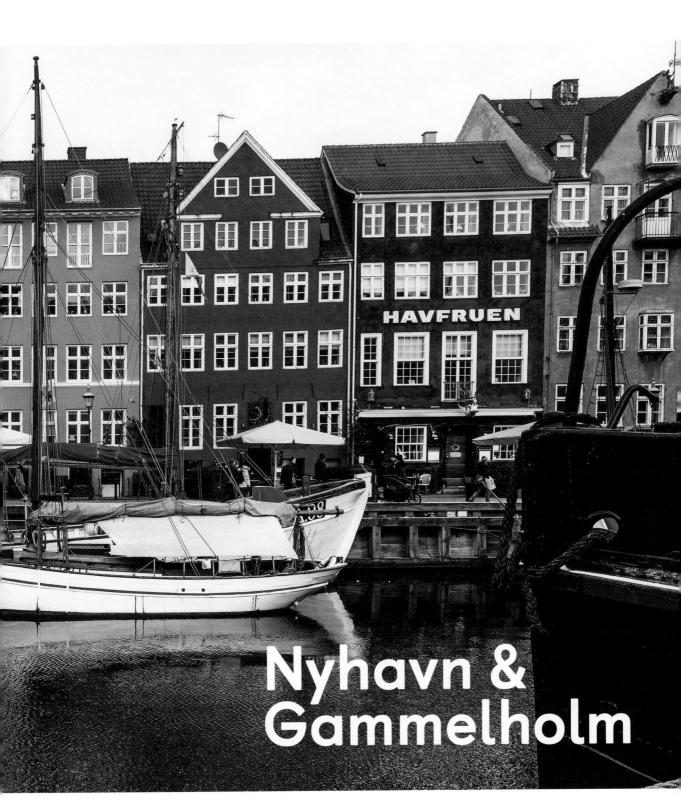

Nyhavn & Gammelholm

When I was about 10 years old, we moved into the Gammelholm neighbourhood, encircled by canals and harbours, where I stayed until I left home as a young adult. Our first residence was a grand apartment with three living rooms and a long corridor with bedrooms branching off on each side. At the end was my room, facing the main street, Holbergsgade.

I could sit on my windowsill and follow the street life beneath me. In those days, lots of folk still lived in central Copenhagen and the streets were lively, full of people doing their daily shopping. All of that was to change rapidly in the years to come, as Copenhagen went through major transformations.

Several other families with children lived in our building, so I soon made new friends. On the fourth floor, above me to the right, lived my friend Tine. I loved being with her family, wrapped in their great traditions. We often had afternoon tea at Tine's house and it was always served with honey bombs. I was very much into all their little rituals, the tea coming in on a tray, Tine's mum pouring it out as we sat around on the smart furniture. The recipe is on the next page, or you can buy them at Perch's tea room in the city centre (page 135).

After some years in that first home, we moved to a new apartment in the next block along, on a different street. At that time, the backyard of each block in this district would be built up with even more blocks of small flats, so the area was very densely populated. That was good for a lot of things as far as I was concerned, especially for the sheer diversity. Lots of different people lived here, there were bustling shops on the main street that sold more unusual foods than the everyday staples and there were children playing everywhere.

However, many of the backyard flats in which these families lived needed renovation. They didn't have bathrooms and they were small and dark. They were all torn down in the 1980s and the people moved to new homes in the suburbs. The backyards were transformed into big new open spaces, bringing in air and light.

In that apartment block, I played with a girl who had long blonde hair, and whose mum always served English toast with butter. Then there was Susie in 7b. Her father was Italian and cooked every morning before he went to work in an Italian restaurant. In their house, I first tasted fried aubergine. He would call me – in Italian – into the kitchen, while Susie would protest, embarrassed, thinking I wouldn't like this exotic thing he had cooked and which most Danish children had never heard of. Susie's dad would pick out slices of aubergines from sizzling olive oil with a fork, leave them to rest for a few minutes on a piece of kitchen paper, then sprinkle them with salt, hand a slice to me and watch and nod slowly while I savoured the great little delight.

Holbergsgade is the main thoroughfare in the Gammelholm area and it used to have a range of small independent food shops. There was the *ismageriet*, the 'dairy', that sold milk, butter and the Danish morning cheese called **Danbo**. It was open from early morning until around 2P.M. Then there were the greengrocer, the sweet shop, the pharmacy and the chocolate shop. On the corner was a shop selling wine, canned food, coffee, tea and dried goods. Like most people, our family had an account here with *købmanden*, the 'merchant', that would be settled every month. I was not allowed to buy anything except when I was expressly sent down to the shop by my father. Naturally, I did not obey this rule, and indeed broke it more often than I am willing to admit, even today! I would often buy myself a *mazarin*, a marzipan cake with chocolate glaze. It was factory made and came in a plastic bag. I still love it, except that now I prefer the homemade variety.

Pages 10–11, and opposite: Nyhavn

Honey bombs

Copenhageners have a long tradition of different honey cakes. If you're in the city, you can buy delicious honey bombs at Perch's tea room (page 135), but if you're far away, bake these, spread them thickly with good salted butter and eat them with a cup of tea.

Makes 16–18

150g [½ cup] honey
150g [¾ cup] soft brown sugar
150g [⅔ cup] salted butter
4 medium eggs
300g [2¼ cups] plain [all-purpose] flour
2 tsp bicarbonate of soda [baking soda]
4 tsp ground cinnamon
3 tsp ground cloves
200g [7oz] candied mixed peel

Preheat the oven to 180°C/350°F/Gas 4.

Gently melt the honey, sugar and butter in a saucepan. Leave the mixture to cool a little, then beat in the eggs one by one.

In a separate large bowl, sift the flour, bicarbonate of soda and spices, then stir this into the honey mixture and add the mixed peel.

Divide the batter between tartlet tins, each 8–9cm [3¼–3½in] in diameter, so that it lies about 1cm [⅛in] deep (you will probably have to bake these in batches).

Bake for 20–25 minutes until well risen and browned, then leave to cool on a wire rack while you cook the rest.

Aubergine salad

My childhood friend Susie's father gave me my first ever fried aubergine.
I have loved it ever since and explored using them in everyday cooking.

Serves 4

For the salad
1 large aubergine [eggplant]
regular olive oil, to brush
sea salt and freshly ground
    black pepper
2 tomatoes, chopped
100g [3½oz] Parmesan cheese,
    grated
6 Tbsp finely chopped curly
    parsley
4 Tbsp chopped dill

For the dressing
1 Tbsp lemon juice
1 tsp apple cider vinegar
2 Tbsp extra virgin olive oil

Cut the aubergine into 1cm [⅜in] slices, then brush them with regular olive oil and sprinkle with salt and pepper. Heat a griddle pan or frying pan until hot. Griddle or fry the slices on both sides for 1–2 minutes on each side.

Place the aubergine slices on a serving dish with the tomatoes. Mix the Parmesan, parsley and dill in a bowl and season with salt and pepper.

Whisk all the ingredients for the dressing together, season with salt and pepper and drizzle it over the aubergines and tomatoes. Scatter the Parmesan mixture over the top and serve right away.

Meat patties (Krebinetter)

A classic Danish dish made from minced meat – half pork and half veal. My grandmother served this with gravy and boiled potatoes but over the years, I have tried to spice the old recipe up a little.

Serves 4

For the krebinetter
250g [9oz] minced [ground] pork
250g [9oz] minced [ground] beef
sea salt and freshly ground
    black pepper
50g [⅓ cup] rye flour
2 Tbsp olive oil
12 sage leaves

For the Jerusalem artichokes
500g [1lb 2oz] Jerusalem
    artichokes
2 Tbsp olive oil

For the cavolo nero
500g [1lb 2oz] cavolo nero,
    stripped from its coarse stalks
2 Tbsp olive oil
1 Tbsp salted butter

For the pea purée
1 Tbsp olive oil
1 shallot, finely chopped
400g [14oz] frozen peas,
    defrosted

Preheat the oven to 180°C/350°F/Gas 4.

For the krebinetter, mix the 2 kinds of meat in a bowl and season well with salt and pepper. Form into 4 patties. Put the rye flour on a plate and turn the burgers in the flour to coat.

For the Jerusalem artichokes, rinse the artichokes well and cut into long slices, with the skins on. Place in a roasting pan lined with baking parchment, toss with the olive oil and some salt and pepper and roast for 20 minutes.

For the cavolo nero, rinse the cavolo nero and drain well. Heat the oil and butter in a saucepan, add the cavolo nero and sauté for 5 minutes. Season to taste with salt and pepper and mix with the Jerusalem artichokes.

Meanwhile, heat the oil in a frying pan and fry the patties for 6–7 minutes on each side over a medium heat. At the same time, fry the sage leaves until crispy. Keep warm.

For the pea purée, heat the oil in a saucepan and sauté the chopped shallot until tender, then add the peas and mix well. Blend the peas and shallot with a blender and season to taste with salt and pepper.

Serve the krebinetter topped with the sage leaves, along with the Jerusalem artichokes and cavolo nero and pea purée.

Mazarin cakes with chocolate glaze

I loved this cake – which I bought at the corner shop as a child – so very much that it is curious that it has taken me more than 30 years to make a homemade version! You will need silicone (or regular) mini-muffin moulds, about 3cm [1¼in] in diameter.

Makes 24

For the cakes
250g [1 cup plus 2 Tbsp] softened salted butter, plus more for the moulds
250g [9oz] marzipan, at least 60% almonds (see page 82 for homemade), grated
250g [1¼ cups] caster [granulated] sugar
5 medium eggs
70g [½ cup] plain [all-purpose] flour
50g [2oz] dark [bittersweet] chocolate, finely chopped, to decorate

To temper the chocolate
200g [7oz] dark [bittersweet] chocolate, broken into pieces

Preheat the oven to 190°C/375°F/Gas 5. If you have regular mini-muffin moulds, you will need to butter them lightly.

For the cakes, beat the grated marzipan with the sugar in a mixing bowl (you will get the best result using an electric mixer), then add the butter and beat again until smooth. Add the eggs one at a time, beating between additions, until the mixture is even and smooth, then fold in the flour.

Transfer the mixture to a piping [pastry] bag and pipe into the mini-muffin moulds (or just use a spoon if you don't have a piping bag). Fill the moulds to just below the rim.

Bake in the oven for 10 minutes, then remove and leave to cool in the moulds.

Now to temper the chocolate. For this you will need a sugar thermometer. Melt 140g [5oz] of the chocolate in a heatproof bowl over a saucepan of simmering water; make sure the bowl does not touch the water. When the chocolate has reached 50°C [122°F], remove the pan from the heat and add the remaining 60g [2oz] chocolate. Mix well until melted. Gently heat in the same way as before until the chocolate reaches 31°C [88°F]. Now it is ready to use. Keep the chocolate's temperature at a steady 31°C [88°F] while you are working with it.

Take the cakes out of the moulds, dip the top of each one in the tempered chocolate and sprinkle with the finely chopped chocolate to decorate.

Nyhavn: the 'dodgy' side

Nyhavn has its share of iconic buildings and is often presented as a Copenhagen landmark. It is a funny place, a mixed bag. I grew up just around the corner, played in the streets and walked here often, on both the so-called 'dodgy' and genteel sides. Hans Christian Andersen lived at several addresses in Nyhavn and wrote some of his famous fairy tales there.

During the '70s and '80s, Nyhavn was in a real decline. On the shadier side, sailors and marines with money to burn used to hang out. The pubs were open 24:7, and there were tattoo parlours and shops selling sailors' equipment. It was smelly but charming, with blinking lights and Danish folk music blaring out each time a pub door opened, either from a juke box or some soloist who played the same songs night after night. You won't find much of this world left, as there has been an invasion of pavement cafés with cosy chairs, blankets and oversized glasses of Chardonnay.

When I was 15, in 1979, I got my first job on the corner of **Nyhavn** and **Toldbodgade**, in a new ice-cream shop. I worked there for the summer and made a lot of money for a young teen. With my first salary, I bought a pair of Fiorucci jeans at a shop called Frk Jensen in the city centre. I felt grown up and independent. The ice-cream shop is still there and remains just as busy as it always was.

Nyhavn means 'new harbour'. The canal, completed by 1671, connects Christian V's New Square – the 'King's Square', which has a grand statue of him – with the open water. It brought merchants closer to the city and with them trade and prosperity to Copenhagen and the whole kingdom of Denmark. The merchants had their houses built next to where their ships were moored and thus a whole new neighbourhood – with warehouses, private houses and a thriving community – was born.

This ended when the English bombed Copenhagen in 1807 and captured the Danish fleet. Nyhavn lay empty, the merchants abandoned it and the sailors moved in. The area lost its grand status, despite its closeness to Amalienborg palace where the Royal family resided (and still does, see page 46).

The beautiful merchants' houses are still there, forming a district of premium apartments. I prefer the sunny side near the end of the canal, which has a view across to **Holmen** (page 94).

In the 1980s, the whole area was renovated and transformed into a pedestrian zone. The pubs became restaurants with outdoor seating and you can now sit on the old quayside along the waterfront and enjoy a beer and admire the scenery. However, there is still one fruitier establishment left as evidence of the good old times: **Hong Kong**. If you are brave enough – and want to try another side of Copenhagen – go there at 9A.M. for a beer with people who haven't gone home yet, or others who need to start the day with an early tipple!

Nyhavn today is both for Danes and tourists, the epitome of Danish *hygge*, with sunshine, high spirits and cold drinks. Near the end of the canal you will find a range of restaurants, including **Hummer**. *Hummer* is Danish for 'lobster'. On a breezy summer day, go and sit outside and enjoy the Danish way of eating *hummer* with a glass of white wine along with the view across the harbour. **Nyhavn 71** nearby is a high-end hotel in a perfect location where you can wake up to the sound of the sea.

The Royal Theatre

On the ground floor of my childhood apartment block was a watchmaker's shop run by a very friendly couple, the Brorsons. I was often invited into their back room for biscuits and a chat, then I started stopping by almost every other day. Afternoons could sometimes drag, so these visits became a welcome ritual and gave me a sense of belonging in the neighbourhood.

The Brorsons knew everybody in Holmen, the area where we lived and where the Royal Theatre is located. Many actors and stagehands also lived in our neighbourhood and often visited the watchmaker's shop, too, handing out free tickets for seats at the top-level gallery.

I remember the first time I was given tickets. I was so thrilled because I had never been to the Royal Theatre... or to any theatre for that matter. I dressed up in the same outfit each time I went: a white shirt with ruffles and a long black velvet skirt. It was thrilling to go, even though it was a bit scary on my own. I was entering unknown territory. In a way, I was playing a part in a script as well: a lucky girl who had dressed up to go to the theatre. I pretended to know everything that was going on, while I looked and listened intently and learned fast how to behave.

Most importantly, I was captivated by the performances, both the opera and the ballet, but ballet especially was easy for me to understand, with its lovely dresses, simple stories and exceptional dancing. This joy in ballet has stayed with me. The Royal Danish Ballet tradition is built on the school of the 19th-century Danish choreographer August Bournonville; one of his famous ballets is called *Napoli* and I can't count how many times I have seen it. I recommend a night in the old theatre to get a sense of the magic and enjoy the excellent Royal Danish Ballet.

The Royal Theatre opened in 1748 and was rebuilt several times during the next 100 years. It has been a stage for live performances ever since. The writer Hans Christian Andersen attempted to become an actor there, around 1820, and also tried to have a play he had written accepted. He failed with both, but he became a protégé of the director of the theatre, Mr Collins, who helped him through his first difficult years in Copenhagen.

In the 1970s, the Royal Theatre had two stages, an old and a new, and they housed four art forms under the same roof: orchestral music, theatre, opera and ballet. In the early 2000s, these were split up between several locations. There is still the old stage, but in addition two new theatres have been constructed close to the old site: **Skuespilhuset** (the Playhouse, pictured left on page 28) and, across the harbour, the **Opera**.

Hakkebøf with hasselback potatoes

You can't get much more Danish than this!
Hasselback potatoes are enjoying a well-deserved revival.

Serves 4

For the hasselback potatoes
12–16 medium potatoes
40g [3 Tbsp] salted butter
4 Tbsp olive oil
coarse sea salt

For the hamburger and onions
about 55g [4 Tbsp] salted butter
2 large onions, sliced
2 Tbsp water
sea salt and freshly ground
 black pepper
300g [10½oz] chanterelle
 mushrooms
600g [1lb 5oz] good-quality
 minced [ground] beef

For the beetroot
2 Tbsp balsamic vinegar
1 tsp honey
400g [14oz] beetroot [beet],
 peeled and grated

Preheat the oven to 200°C/400°F/Gas 6.

For the hasselback potatoes, first peel the potatoes. Lay each on a long side and make vertical cuts across them, at 3mm [⅛in] intervals almost right through, but not quite. Heat the butter and oil in a saucepan until sizzling, but not turning brown. Place the potatoes in a roasting pan, cut side up, and pour the butter mixture over, making sure it coats the potatoes and that the bottom of the tin is covered, too. Sprinkle each potato with coarse salt. Bake for 40–50 minutes, testing to see whether they are tender, basting 2 or 3 times during baking.

Meanwhile, for the hamburger and onions, melt half the butter in a saucepan. Add the sliced onions and fry them over a medium-low heat until golden brown. Increase the heat, add the water and ½ tsp salt and continue frying until the liquid has reduced. Remove from the saucepan and keep warm.

Clean the chanterelles well with a dry brush, fry in about 1 Tbsp butter until golden brown, then add to the softened onions.

Form 4 burgers from the beef and sprinkle each side with salt and pepper. Melt the last of the butter in the frying pan and fry the burgers on both sides until medium-rare, or more well-done if you prefer.

For the beetroot, whisk the balsamic vinegar and honey together, stir in the grated beetroot, then season to taste with salt and pepper.

Serve the hamburgers with the soft onions and chanterelles piled on top, and the hasselback potatoes and beetroot on the side.

Lobster salad

Buying a whole live lobster will ensure that the meat is fresh, but it does mean that you will have to kill it, which is not a job for the squeamish. Lobsters have to smell very fresh and still be lively when you pick them up: if you straighten out their tails, they should swiftly curve them back under their bodies.

Serves 4

2 lobsters

For the brine
5 litres [quarts] water
juice of 1 lemon
3 dill sprigs
1 Tbsp sea salt

For the vinaigrette
1 Tbsp finely chopped shallots
4 Tbsp lemon juice
2 Tbsp extra virgin olive oil
1 tsp honey
sea salt and freshly ground
    black pepper

For the salad
2 heads of white chicory [endive]
1 fennel bulb
1 Tbsp salted butter
10 dill sprigs
bunch of watercress

For the brine, take a large pot and pour in the water, then add the lemon juice, dill and salt. Bring it to the boil over a high heat.

Kill the lobsters: take a sharp knife, pierce the point into the heads and swiftly make a cut down through the shells. Add the lobsters to the boiling water and boil for 8 minutes, then take them out of the water, stretch out the tails so that they are straight and let them cool down.

Meanwhile, whisk all the ingredients for the vinaigrette together until well combined.

Now, for the salad, take the meat out of the lobster shells and claws, and cut it into smaller pieces. Cut the heads of chicory lengthways into thin wedges. Cut the fennel super-fine and place it in ice-cold water so that it curls up.

Melt the butter in a frying pan and fry the chicory wedges on each side. Place them in 4 dishes, then arrange the pieces of lobster in between. Drizzle with the dressing and decorate with the fennel, dill and watercress. Sprinkle with pepper and serve right away.

Choux pastry buns (Marieboller)

A classic choux pastry filled with cream and, here, a bit of lemon.
These buns are not difficult to make and are a winner every time.

Serves 6

For the craquelin

150g [⅔ cup] softened unsalted butter

175g [¾ cup plus 2 Tbsp] caster [granulated] sugar

175g [1⅓ cups] plain [all-purpose] flour

30g [½ cup] desiccated [shredded] coconut, toasted

For the choux pastry

100g [7 Tbsp] unsalted butter, plus more for the sheet

200ml [¾ cup] water

100g [¾ cup] plain [all-purpose] flour

½ tsp caster [granulated] sugar

pinch of fine sea salt

3 medium eggs, lightly beaten

For the cream

300ml [1¼ cups] double [heavy] cream

50g [5 Tbsp] icing [confectioner's] sugar, plus more to dust

2 Tbsp grated unwaxed lemon zest

Start with the craquelin. Mix all the ingredients together and mix well.

Preheat the oven to 200°C/400°F/Gas 6.

For the choux pastry, put the butter in a saucepan with the water and let it melt over a gentle heat. Now increase the heat and bring to the boil. Meanwhile, sift the flour, sugar and salt into a bowl. Reduce the heat under the saucepan, add the flour mixture and stir with a wooden spoon until a firm, smooth paste is formed. Beat until it comes away from the sides of the pan and forms a ball, then remove from the heat and leave to cool for 10 minutes.

Add the eggs to the dough a little at a time, beating well after each addition, until the mixture is smooth and glossy. (You may not need all the egg.)

Line a baking sheet with baking parchment. Using 2 spoons, form little balls of dough the size of walnuts and arrange on the parchment, leaving about 2cm [¾in] between each. Use up all the dough.

Put the craquelin mixture between 2 sheets of baking parchment and roll with a rolling pin until the mixture is about 2mm [⅛in] thick. Freeze for 3 minutes, or until cold and stiff. Now cut out squares about 3cm [1¼in] wide and place one over each choux ball.

Bake for 35–40 minutes; do not open the oven door for the first 20 minutes of cooking or the pastry might not rise. Remove from the oven and leave the buns to cool on a wire rack.

Meanwhile, for the cream, whip the cream with the sugar until light and fluffy, then fold in the lemon zest. Cut each choux bun in half and spoon some of the whipped cream on the bottom half. Top with the craquelin lid, dust with icing sugar and serve right away.

Nyhavn: the genteel side

On the so-called 'proper' side of Nyhavn is **Kunsthal Charlottenborg**, the gallery attached to the **Royal Academy**, an art school that has been on this site since 1754. When I was a child, my father went to the school of architecture, which was part of the Academy, and has also exhibited there, so I have spent a lot of time in the old buildings. They are beautiful. Charlottenborg has really great exhibitions, featuring both Danish and international artists. Each year there is a Spring Exhibition and I always try to go. I remember visiting as a child and gazing at the enormous sculptures. You turn a corner off bustling, noisy Nyhavn… and find yourself in this great big square, grand and almost empty. I always feel peace enveloping me as soon as I enter. You can hear the wind and feel the sun; it is a true breathing space in the city. In summer there is a café here, where you can sit outside.

The genteel side of Nyhavn has been extended by a new **bicycle bridge**, opened in 2016, that crosses the harbour waters and connects **Nyhavn** with **Holmen** and **Christianshavn** (pages 94 and 81). It has changed the district profoundly and, every time I cross the bridge on my bike or on foot, I am excited to experience my home town in a new way. It has given life to the neighbourhood I grew up in, improved the infrastructure of the city and made it even more evident that Copenhagen is a bicycling town.

In the restaurants in this area you'll find a lot of classic dishes such as *smørrebrød*, together with light French dishes with a Danish twist. There is **Cap Horn**, which is a very famous pub (see below) and now a restaurant with a modern Danish kitchen.

Many of the restaurants serve steak; this started in the 1980s when the ubiquitous, tasteless steak with pepper sauce and potatoes became a big deal. For a traditional Danish beef dish, go for the old-fashioned roast beef with gravy, potatoes and green beans, served with lingonberry or redcurrant jelly and sweet-and-sour cucumber salad.

Værtshuse

The word for pub in Denmark is *værtshus*, which literally means 'host's house'. There used to be several in each area, and most people had a preferred regular. *Værtshuse* became regulated by law in 1857, as they were an important part of life in Copenhagen. They served alcohol all day. You could eat your lunch there – either food you brought with you from home or lunch or dinner that they served there. In the morning, the *værtshus* would sell milk toddy, which was raw milk with aquavit… that's the way to start your day!

Top left: Nyhavnbroen. Top right and bottom: Bicycle bridge connecting Nyhavn with Holmen and Christianhavn. Just over the bridge is Copenhagen street food market.

Classic roasted beef with gravy

You want a classic, old-school Danish roast, served well done? Here it is. I have just modernized it a little, adding root vegetables to the potatoes.

Serves 8

For the meat
2.5kg [5½lb] chuck steak
sea salt and freshly ground
    black pepper
5 thyme sprigs
500ml [2 cups] water
1 parsnip
5 turnips
1kg [2¼lb] small potatoes
3 onions
1 garlic bulb
redcurrant jelly, to serve

For the gravy
25g [2 Tbsp] salted butter
1 onion, chopped
1 carrot, chopped
10 thyme sprigs
2 bay leaves
2 Tbsp plain [all-purpose] flour
200ml [¾ cup] red wine
800ml [3⅓ cups] beef stock
200ml [1 cup] double [heavy]
    cream

Preheat the oven to 200°C/400°F/Gas 6.

For the meat, rub the steak with salt and pepper and place in a roasting pan. Tuck half the thyme sprigs under the meat. Put it into the oven. After the first 10 minutes, pour the water into the roasting pan, then continue to roast for a total of 1½ hours.

Meanwhile, peel the parsnip; wash the turnips and cut both into chunks; wash the potatoes and cut them in half along with the peel-on onions and garlic. Mix all the vegetables in a large bowl, seasoning with salt and pepper.

After the meat has been roasting for 1½ hours, take it out of the oven, add the vegetables to the roasting pan and mix them well with the juices, then roast everything for another hour.

Meanwhile, for the gravy, melt the butter in a saucepan and sauté the chopped onion and carrot, the thyme and bay leaves. After a few minutes, add the flour and mix well, then pour in the red wine and stock. Leave it to simmer for 30 minutes, stirring occasionally, then strain it into a clean saucepan. Add the cream and season to taste with salt and pepper.

When the roast is done, serve it with the gravy and redcurrant jelly.

'Burning love' with beetroot

A true classic, though I have tweaked the traditional recipe a little,
adding beetroot to the bacon, instead of eating it, pickled, on the side.
If you don't want the meat, replace the bacon with walnuts.

Serves 4

For the mash
1kg [2¼lb] floury potatoes
sea salt and freshly ground
    black pepper
25g [2 Tbsp] salted butter
100ml [⅓ cup] whole milk, warmed
½ tsp freshly grated nutmeg

For the topping
400g [14oz] smoked streaky
    bacon, finely chopped
4 onions, chopped
200g [7oz] beetroot [beet],
    peeled and finely chopped
1 celery stick, finely chopped
leaves from a bunch of curly
    parsley, finely chopped

For the mash, peel and cut the potatoes into big chunks. Boil them in salted water until tender. Drain them, reserving some of the cooking liquid. Mash the potatoes with a balloon whisk until they are the texture you prefer. Add the butter and warm milk, stirring until the butter has melted, then season to taste with salt, pepper and the nutmeg. Splash in some of the cooking liquid if you would like a looser mash.

Meanwhile, for the topping, fry the bacon in a frying pan over a medium heat in its own fat until golden and crispy. Remove from the pan using a slotted spoon, leaving the fat in the pan. Add the onions, beetroot and celery to the fat in the pan and fry until golden brown, then return the bacon and season with pepper.

Serve the mash with the bacon and beetroot, onions and celery on top, all sprinkled with the parsley.

Store Strandstræde and Lille Strandstræde

In all the cities of the world, there are secret pockets: take a few steps away from the main tourist drag and little gems are to be found that give a place its real character. When it comes to the area around Nyhavn, these jewels are the two small back streets called **Lille Strandstræde** and **Store Strandssträde**. They have beautiful houses, boutique shops, bakeries, wine bars and cafés, and the two streets connect in a very small romantic square.

At Store Strandstræde you'll find **Café Zeleste**, a small café in an old quirky house with a very romantic backyard where you can sit outside. Danes would describe this place as very *hyggeligt*. It is a 1980s icon, one of the very first cafés in Copenhagen to serve reliably good food made from great-quality produce. In the 1980s, I ate many goat cheese salads here, and when my children were small, I'd bring them here as a treat for a weekend breakfast. Also *hyggeligt* is **Nebbiolo**, a wine bar that celebrates good Italian wine and charcuterie.

The square leads to **Sankt Annæ Plads**, which up until recently was abandoned and a touch anonymous. You would find few tourists except at **Restaurant Sankt Annæ**, which serves a classic Danish lunch and has a solid crew of regulars. I hung out there as a teenager, when we would bike, roller-skate and skateboard. These days the square has been totally renovated. There's a playground, benches, new wide pavement and smart cafés. The development seems to have magicked people out of rabbit holes, because now they are everywhere.

At the end of Sankt Annæ Plads is the **waterfront** – again a newly renovated quay – and a big wooden public porch with swimming access to the harbour water. In the winter you'll find sauna clubs and jacuzzi boats. (Yes, we crazy Vikings swim all year round.) In the summer there are concerts and morning yoga sessions.

The harbour

I grew up near the harbour. In those days, most of the harbour was not developed; it was a working harbour with goods coming in and out constantly. There were only two passenger ferries then: one for Bornholm and one for Oslo, in Norway. The Bornholm ferries passed in and out uneventfully, but the Oslo ferries would leave at midnight accompanied by a lot of noise from drunk young people shouting silly slogans.

Now, the ferries depart from a different part of the waterway and the central part of Copenhagen harbour has been renovated into public parks and walking and bicycling tracks. The water is clean and the harbour has swimming clubs and designated swimming areas, so the water becomes very lively as soon as the weather allows it.

Opposite: *A Neapolitan Fisherman Teaching His Son to Play the Flute* by Otto Evens, on the corner of Store Strandstræde and Lille Strandstræde

Frederiksstaden

Frederiksstaden is the neighbourhood just north of where I grew up. I always enjoy walking and bicycling here. It was the setting for my daily journey to and from school, meeting friends or hanging out as a teenager. I really feel this area is part of my childhood identity.

It is one of the most beautiful areas in Copenhagen and, walking around here, you really get a sense of the history of the city. Walk along Bredgade down to Grønningen and up Amaliegade, then sneak into some of the small courtyards. If you can find numbers 23–25, you will discover a small museum of medical history – which I have never been in – with its lovely little garden. It feels like a different era. Walk down to the harbour to see the small section of what we call the 'English houses', then head directly to the harbour and take in the statue of Mary Thomas, the rebel leader who protested against the harsh treatment of former slaves in the then-Danish colony of St Croix in the Caribbean. It is impressive and a beautiful statement, but not yet permanent and fundraising continues to ensure that it remains there for all time, in bronze form.

Frederiksstaden is home to Amalienborg Palace, built in the 1750s by Danish architect Nicolai Eigtved. He was also the architect behind the whole Frederiksstaden area that surrounds the palace, and his was a golden era in Copenhagen's architecture. As part of the new district, Frederiksstaden included a hospital for the nobility living there, which is now the Industrial Design Museum, and the famous Marble Church. Here you will also find the Russian Orthodox Church.

Frederiksstaden typically has large houses, built for nobility during the winter season. Later, the higher echelons of bourgeois society moved in. Now, these erstwhile homes are mostly offices, auction houses, antiques shops, jewellers, a piano store, galleries, coffee bars and a few restaurants. It is one of the most beautiful areas in Copenhagen and I love to walk around here. (Be aware that there are few everyday shops – for that you'll have to go a few blocks away.)

The **Industrial Design Museum** is worth a visit, especially if you're into design and fashion. At the café there, you can sit outside and enjoy the beautiful courtyard. In summer, this is the setting for outdoor performances of plays by the Grønnegaards Theatre. The plays are in Danish, so it's probably a long evening if you don't speak the language, but it's a great tradition… as long as it doesn't rain. Before you take your seats for the performance, you can start your evening with a picnic on the grass.

There are a number of churches in Copenhagen that stand out and the **Marble Church** (Frederiks Kirke) is one of them. It's beautiful from the outside, of course, but the real attraction is going up inside the dome to the viewing platform to enjoy the view over **Amalienborg Palace** all the way down to the other side of the harbour. On a clear day it is quite breathtaking and you may even be able to see all the way across to Sweden.

The Marble Church took 145 years to finish, from 1749 to 1894. After several architects tried and failed to complete the job, and a lack of money for the work, it was finally taken over by locally famous Danish industrialist CF Tietgen. He stumped up the necessary cash and hired the architect Ferdinand Meldalh to design it, inspired by St Peter's Basilica in Rome. It is an impressive church, though there remains an ongoing debate about whether people love it or hate it. I think the dome is beautiful and that the view from it gives a great perspective of the city as well as lending some grandness to Copenhagen.

Pages 42–44: Bridge to Kastellet
Opposite: Marble Church

Amalienborg

This is the main palace in Copenhagen and it is where the royal family lives. I think the square is magical. I like to go there at night and enjoy the winking street lights and the silence. Yes, silence. There's a weird calm, as though the history of the place shuts out the modern world and lets you just exist. At least, until the occasional noise from somebody driving over the cobbled square reminds you that this is part of a living city.

I like to stand in the square, take a deep breath and enjoy its magic. When it snows, it's my favourite place in Copenhagen, especially at night when the snow is new and fresh, and untouched. I have walked over the cobbles at all times of day and in all seasons. I never just pass by; I always make time to take it in. In my world, it is perfect.

Clockwise from top right: Frederick VIII's Palace; the royal guards; red sentry boxes outside the palaces

Tartlets with mushrooms in cream

Tartlets can be complicated to make,
so I have made this recipe a bit easier.

Makes 8; serves 4

For the tartlets
500g [1lb 2oz] ready-made
   all-butter puff pastry
plain [all-purpose] flour, to dust
1 egg, lightly beaten

For the filling
500g [1lb 2oz] mushrooms
10g [2 tsp] salted butter
1 garlic clove, finely chopped
3 thyme sprigs
200ml [1 cup] crème fraîche
juice of 1 lemon, or to taste
sea salt and freshly ground
   black pepper
leaves from a small bunch of
   flat-leaf parsley, chopped

Preheat the oven to 180°C/350°F/Gas 4.

For the tartlets, roll out the puff pastry on a lightly floured surface to about 5mm [¼in] thick and cut out 16 rectangles. Score a lattice pattern over the tops of 8 of the rectangles and make these the 'lids'. Brush all the rectangles with the beaten egg. Place them on a baking sheet and bake for 15–20 minutes until light golden brown. Take out of the oven and leave on a wire rack.

Meanwhile, for the filling, rinse the mushrooms carefully, pat dry and cut them into slices. Melt the butter in a frying pan and sauté the garlic, thyme and mushrooms for 10 minutes. Add the crème fraîche and let it simmer, stirring, until the cream has thickened. Season to taste with the lemon juice, salt and pepper.

Spoon the hot mushroom cream over the bottoms of the pastry rectangles and sprinkle with the parsley. Top with the lids and serve at once.

Chicken liver pâté with aquavit

The late Prince Consort Henrik, who died in 2018, was French by birth and known for his interest in food and cooking. He wrote cookbooks and always had a say in the daily menu of the Royal Court. I cooked for him a few times during my time running the restaurant in the Danish Parliament and, on one occasion, I made him this pâté. He came over and asked how I had done it. So this is the answer!

Serves 8

For the pâté

1 Tbsp salted butter, plus 250g
  [1 cup plus 2 Tbsp] more chilled
  salted butter, cubed
2 shallots, finely chopped
2 whole cloves
1kg [2¼lb] chicken livers, trimmed
  and halved
10 thyme sprigs
200ml [¾ cup] aquavit
250ml [1 cup] crème fraîche
sea salt and freshly ground
  black pepper

To serve

lingonberry jam
rye bread (see page 264
  for homemade), toasted

For the pâté, melt the 1 Tbsp butter in a large saucepan, add the shallots and cloves and sauté until soft. Add the chicken livers and thyme sprigs and cook for 5 minutes, stirring occasionally. Add the aquavit, then increase the heat and simmer for 5 minutes. Turn off the heat and leave the mixture in the saucepan for 5 minutes.

Take out the thyme sprigs and cloves, then transfer the chicken liver mixture to a food processor. Add the 250g [1 cup plus 2 Tbsp] cubed butter and the crème fraîche and blend until smooth. Season to taste with salt and pepper. Pour the pâté mixture into a terrine mould or loaf tin and refrigerate until the next day.

Serve the pâté with lingonberry jam and rye bread.

Lumskebugten

This is Denmark's oldest restaurant. It has a colourful history, told in a little booklet you can pick up if you dine there. The restaurant is divided into separate old-style dining rooms, without seeming outdated at all. This is quintessential *hygge*, so if you want to experience Danish *hygge* and the best of Danish cuisine, this is the place to eat. I go for lunch often and also like to take my foreign friends to experience true Danish food culture. The *smørrebrød* is classic, but with a modern flavour.

The owner, Erwin Lauterbach, understands tradition without being burdened by it, and renews it in his own subtle ways. Lauterbach is a highly respected Danish chef, in many ways one of the godfathers of the modern Danish kitchen, I believe. I have tremendous respect for him. I once asked Erwin why he started cooking with local fish and vegetables. His answer was very pragmatic: in the '70s, when he worked in a restaurant in Malmö, he was tired of having to bring in French produce on board the ferry from Copenhagen every day. One day he went to the market instead and decided to buy the local celeriac and leeks, and started putting them on his menu. Then he began collaborating with local producers and finding out more about what the local terroir can offer.

Erwin's cooking is classic and always seasonal. Through his many TV shows, books and newspaper columns he has reminded us of what the seasons really mean, and of the importance of our own terroir. My mother-in-law would cut out his columns and put them in binders for me with her own remarks here and there. It is like she is still with me in the kitchen.

Eating is not only about flavour and well-balanced meals. It is also about the ritual, how the table is set, the choice of china, glasses, flowers and so on. At Lumskebugten, it is clear that they celebrate tradition, but also that things move on with time. The service is old-school and at the same time *hyggelig*, which inherently means you just feel at home. The signature dishes are warm smoked herring with egg yolk, calf's tongue with sweetbreads and fishcakes with homemade rémoulade, all beautifully done. In the following pages are some other dishes inspired by Erwin.

Opposite: Erwin Lauterbach. Above: Lumskebugten

Seared cod roe with Trine's mayo

Cod roe is in season in the winter, when you will find it on the menu at all the classic *smørrebrød* venues, served either with mayonnaise or rémoulade.

Serves 4

For the brine

1 litre [4¼ cups] water

½ Tbsp coarse sea salt

1 Tbsp black peppercorns

2 slices of lemon

For the smørrebrød

200g [7oz] fresh (unsmoked) cod roe

25g [2 Tbsp] salted butter

4 slices of rye bread (see page 264 for homemade)

dill sprigs, to serve

sea salt and freshly ground black pepper

8 thin slices of lemon

For the rémoulade

1 carrot, finely sliced

120g [4oz] celeriac [celery root], peeled and finely chopped

sea salt

½ cucumber, deseeded and cut into tiny dice

50ml [3½ Tbsp] good mayonnaise (see page 56 for homemade)

½ tsp finely grated red onion

1 tsp medium curry powder

½ tsp English mustard powder

1 tsp lemon juice

2 Tbsp capers, drained, rinsed and chopped

First make the brine. Bring the water to the boil in a saucepan, then add the salt, peppercorns and lemon slices. Reduce the heat to a simmer. Place the roe in the brine and simmer for 30 minutes. Remove the roe from the water with a slotted spoon and leave to cool.

Meanwhile, make the rémoulade. Boil the carrot and celeriac in lightly salted water for 4–5 minutes. Drain and leave to cool, then mix with the cucumber in a bowl.

In another bowl, mix together the mayonnaise, onion, curry and mustard powders, lemon juice and capers, then mix this into the carrot and celeriac mixture.

For the smørrebrød, cut the cold cod roe into 1.5cm [⅝in]-thick slices with a sharp knife. Heat the butter in a frying pan over a medium heat and sear the roe on both sides until light golden.

Place the roe on the slices of bread, then add about 2–3 Tbsp rémoulade on top of each. Season with salt and pepper, top with dill sprigs and serve with the lemon slices.

Prawns with dill

When I have time, I like to peel the prawns myself. I love to buy several kilos of them, invite people over and have a long lunch, everyone peeling them for their own *smørrebrød*. Yes, it is a bit fussy, but it tastes so much better!

Serves 4

40g [3 Tbsp] good mayonnaise
  (see below)
½ Tbsp lemon juice
300g [10½oz] good-quality cooked
  peeled prawns [shrimp]
4 large slices of rye bread (see
  page 264 for homemade)
1 asparagus
freshly ground black pepper
handful of dill sprigs
1 lemon, sliced

Mix the mayonnaise and lemon juice together in a small bowl. Place the prawns on the bread, then spoon the lemon mayonnaise. Shave the asparagus into ribbons with a vegetable peeler.

Put the asparagus on the mayonnaise. Sprinkle with pepper, add the dill and serve with lemon slices.

Classic mayonnaise

Makes 300ml [1¼ cups]

2 egg yolks
1 Tbsp Dijon mustard
1 tsp white wine vinegar
250ml [1 cup] flavourless
  cold-pressed oil
¼ tsp sea salt
freshly ground black pepper

Whisk the egg yolks in a bowl, then add the mustard and vinegar and whisk together for 5 minutes. I prefer to use a food processor or electric whisk for this.

Gradually add about half the oil, very slowly at first, whisking constantly, until the mixture is thickened and emulsified. Continue adding the remaining oil gradually, whisking constantly.

Season with the salt and a pinch of pepper. Store in a sterilized jar in the refrigerator for up to 1 week.

Sterilizing jars and bottles: I sterilize glass jars and bottles by pouring boiling water into each, closing them tightly and shaking them well. Pour out the water and they are ready to use.

Lumpfish roe with blinis

A local fish roe you will find in many restaurants around Copenhagen in season, though the season changes every year and could fall any time from from January to May. It is classically served here with blinis, red onion and crème fraîche, but it is also great with boiled potatoes, rye bread or rösti. If you are in the UK, you are probably more familiar with the roe, dyed black, in cans. The fresh, undyed version is a million times better.

Serves 4

For the blinis
150ml [⅔ cup] whole milk
15g [½oz] fresh yeast
2 medium eggs, separated
100g [½ cup] sour cream
70g [½ cup] buckwheat flour
70g [½ cup] strong white flour
½ tsp freshly grated nutmeg
1 tsp fine sea salt
25g [2 Tbsp] salted butter

For the lightly pickled onion
1 small red onion
4 Tbsp lemon juice, plus more for the roe
1 tsp sugar (any type)
sea salt and freshly ground black pepper

To serve
400g [14oz] lumpfish roe, rinsed
200g [1 scant cup] crème fraîche

Start with the blinis. Heat the milk in a small saucepan; when it begins to boil, take it off the heat and stir in the yeast, followed by the egg yolks and the sour cream. Stir the mixture well.

In a separate bowl, mix the flours, nutmeg and salt, then slowly pour in the contents of the saucepan, stirring all the time. When you have a smooth paste, cover and leave in a warm place for 1 hour to prove: it should look a little spongy and develop a few bubbles on the surface.

Whisk the egg whites to soft peaks, then gently fold them into the blini mixture. Leave for another 2 hours to rest.

Meanwhile, lightly pickle the onion. Peel and cut it into 1cm [⅜in] slices, place them in a non-reactive bowl with the lemon juice, sugar, ½ tsp salt and some pepper and let rest for at least 30 minutes.

When ready to cook the blinis, melt the butter in a large frying pan over a medium-high heat, then add the batter, in 1 Tbsp pools, to the pan and cook for 2 minutes. Flip them over and cook for 1–2 minutes or so on the other side, or until golden brown. Keep the cooked blinis warm in a low oven while you cook the rest.

Just before serving, season the roe with lemon juice, salt and pepper. Serve the warm blinis with the roe, crème fraîche and pickled onion.

Turbot with lemon and tarragon

In my opinion, turbot is the king of the sea and tastes heavenly. I first ate it in the late '80s in Erwin Lauterbach's restaurant, Saison. You will often find it on traditional Danish menus in Copenhagen. I like to bake it whole when I have guests for dinner; it is easy, but impressive.

Serves 8

2–2.5kg [4½–5½lb] turbot
sea salt and freshly ground
    black pepper
2 lemons, sliced and cut into
    half moons
6 tarragon sprigs

Preheat the oven to 180°C/350°F/Gas 4.

Cut away the head and the fins on either side of the turbot, then rinse the fish inside and out. Place the turbot on a baking sheet lined with baking parchment. Make 3 cuts on each side of the main bone, each about 1.5cm [⅝in] deep. Sprinkle with salt and pepper and place the lemon slices and tarragon sprigs on top.

Bake in the oven for 20–25 minutes. It is ready when a finger pressed on the spine makes the fillets start to slip away.

Lamb in dill sauce with new potatoes

This just screams summer, with dill,
and new potatoes and carrots.

Serves 4

1kg [2¼lb] small new potatoes,
  roasted, to serve

For the broth
800g [1¾lb] boned lamb shoulder
large bunch of dill, about 150g
  [5½oz]
1 carrot, cut into chunks
1 leek, cut into chunks and
  well rinsed
1 onion, halved
2 bay leaves
6 black peppercorns
1 tsp sea salt

For the dill sauce
100g [½ cup] salted butter
100g [¾ cup] plain [all-purpose]
  flour
2 carrots, cut into thin slices
  at an angle
1 leek, cut into thin slices and
  well rinsed
200ml [¾ cup] double [heavy]
  cream
sea salt and freshly ground
  black pepper

For the broth, cut the lamb shoulder into 3cm [1¼in] cubes. Pick the dill sprigs off the stems and chop them, reserving the stems.

Place the meat in a saucepan, cover with cold water, bring to the boil and cook for 3–4 minutes. Lots of scum will rise to the surface. Pour the meat into a sieve [strainer] and rinse with cold water.

Clean the saucepan, return the meat, then add the dill stems and all the other ingredients for the broth (not the chopped dill; keep that aside). Cover with fresh water. Bring to the boil, then reduce the heat and let simmer for about 1 hour until the meat is tender.

Remove the lamb from the broth with a slotted spoon. Place a piece of muslin [cheesecloth] in a sieve over a clean bowl and pour the broth through. Measure 600ml [2½ cups] of the broth for the dill sauce. (Any leftover broth can be frozen for a lamb gravy or stew.)

For the dill sauce, melt the butter in a heavy-based saucepan, whisk in the flour and cook until foaming. Add the 600ml [2½ cups] strained broth little by little, whisking constantly until boiling. Add the carrots and leek, then simmer for 8–10 minutes. Add the lamb and cream and return to the boil. Turn off the heat, add the chopped dill and season with salt and pepper.

Serve hot with the roasted new potatoes.

Kastellet

In the summer, when I take one of my early-morning walks, I like to visit **Kastellet** a few times each week. It is an old fortress with a moat, by the waterfront that is part of **Frederiksstaden**, not far from **The Little Mermaid statue**. If you could see the fortress from above, you would find that it is star-shaped and you can walk on a path on top of this wall; from there you get a great view over the harbour. The fortress is still used by the Danish military, but is also open to the public.

Kastellet has very beautiful ancient trees and an old windmill. The iconic **Copenhagen benches** (pictured right on page 67) can be found on the pathway all around the star-shaped wall, so bring coffee and cake from one of the nearby bakeries before you enter, then sit here and enjoy the view with a picnic.

Copenhagen is often very windy, even in summer, and you feel it at Kastellet. But in Copenhagen we have a famous saying: 'There's no such thing as bad weather, only the wrong clothing'… so you had better be prepared!

Bicycles

One of the very best things about Copenhagen is that it is so easy to get around. The main reason for that is the bicycle culture. Bikes are the primary form of transport, so when you visit, rent a bike and take a few seconds to understand the rules of the road so that you are not a danger to your fellow cyclists. Locals can spot a tourist on a bike from miles away!

Rhubarb tartlets

I don't think I ever get tired of rhubarb, whether it is in savoury
or sweet recipes. You'll find a lot of dishes with rhubarb in
Copenhagen: sodas, cakes, compote and candy. This tart is made
with rhubarb that is in season in Denmark in June and July. You will
need tartlet tins with removable bases, each 9–10cm [3½–4in] in
diameter, for this recipe. The tartlet cases, without the filling,
keep for 2–3 days in an airtight container.

Makes 8

whipped cream or crème fraîche,
    to serve

For the pastry

50g [⅓ cup] almonds

175g [1⅓ cups] plain [all-purpose]
    flour, plus more to dust

75g [½ cup] icing [confectioner's]
    sugar

75g [⅓ cup] chilled salted butter,
    chopped, plus more for the tins

1 egg, lightly beaten

For the filling

500g [1lb 2oz] rhubarb, cut into
    2cm [¾in] pieces

1 vanilla pod [bean], halved
    lengthways

100g [½ cup] caster [granulated]
    sugar

For the pastry, grind the almonds very finely. Mix the
flour, ground almonds and icing sugar together in a
bowl. Rub in the butter with your fingertips until the
mixture resembles crumbs. Mix in the egg without
over-working the pastry. Wrap in clingfilm [plastic
wrap] and refrigerate for at least 1 hour.

Butter 8 x 9–10cm [3½–4in] tartlet tins carefully. (If
you don't have 8 tins, just bake these in batches.) Roll
the pastry out on a floured work surface to 2mm
[⅛in] thick, then use it to line the tins. Trim off the
excess pastry from the sides of the tin with a knife.
Refrigerate the tins for at least 1 hour, or overnight.

Preheat the oven to 180°C/350°F/Gas 4. Bake the
tarts for 12–14 minutes, then place them on a wire
rack to cool down.

Meanwhile, make the filling. Place the rhubarb in a
saucepan with the vanilla pod and sugar. Bring to the
boil over a medium heat, then reduce the heat and
simmer for 4–5 minutes until the rhubarb pieces are
just tender but still keeping their shape. Remove from
the heat and take out the vanilla pod.

Divide the filling between the baked tartlet cases and
return to the oven for a final 5 minutes. Serve with
whipped cream or crème fraîche.

Hotels

You do not sleep in hotels in the city you live in, for the good reason that you are not in a need of a bed! However, for the purposes of this book, I decided I wanted to have an overnight stay in a favourite hotel in my own city, so I asked a friend to join me to play tourists in our home town for 24 hours. The location of **Hotel Babette** is perfect: central, but in a very green area and close to the harbour. Importantly, they have an organic and sustainable approach to their business that I applaud. Hotel Babette is part of a chain called Guldsmeden, and they have other great hotels in other areas of town.

As soon as I step into the hotel world, I am in a space without everyday time, with no strings attached, and where there is no washing-up or laundry to do. I like to inhabit the space, spread out my belongings and move a few things around for it to feel like mine for the time I am there. I love staying in a good hotel – I relax and regenerate.

After we checked in, we went for a walk along the quay to Amaliehaven, stopping for coffee and cake at the café on Sankt Annæ Square. After our walk, we returned to the hotel and went to the rooftop sauna, taking in the amazing view over Copenhagen. After a good dinner, we slept in very comfortable beds. Even in our own city, it felt like a mini holiday.

As you'd expect in an international capital, there are lots of great hotels in Copenhagen. In the luxury bracket are **Sander**, **Hotel d'Angleterre** or **Nimb** in Tivoli. For quirkiness, at Vesterbro there is the world's smallest hotel – just one room (page 184). **Nyhavn 71** has a great view over the harbour, while **Hotel Kong Artur** is at the lakes. Lower budgets will embrace the modern hostel **Steel House**.

Restaurants

There are many restaurants in Frederiksstaden and nearby: French bistros, classic Danish or Italian places, cafés, burger joints and much more. I recommend **Restaurant Palægade** or **Restaurant Amalie**.

On Bredgade you will find **Salon**, a new place run by the legendary Claus Christensen who is known for his classic Danish/French cooking and for celebrating the Danish seasons. He has a true interest in art and culture, which form part of the experience of eating with him.

Find the secret alley at the end of **Sankt Annæ Plads**, leading from **Bredgade** to **Store Kongensgade**. You will be led on to a small square called **Landgreven** to a petrol station and the **Gasolin Grill**. Get a burger there – it is famous. I have never had one, but only because, though I've stood in the queue a few times, they sold out before I got to the front. I guess you need to get there early!

Kafferiet

Coffee bars are an essential part of Copenhagen life, and a visitor to the city should try a few out. Kafferiet is a quirky and fun small coffee chain. It has its own little universe, painted with lovely colours, accessorized by candy and – most importantly – offering great coffee. It is a bit like Hans Christian Andersen meets Danish design. There are five branches dotted around Copenhagen; pictured opposite is the original one.

Cod with hollandaise

I once made hollandaise on the spot for 20 firefighters on shift – and then the fire alarm went off and they all disappeared! This is easier as it's only for 4 people, so don't worry; just follow the recipe and it will work fine.

Serves 4

For the beetroot and cod
250g [9oz] beetroot [beet]
sea salt and freshly ground
    black pepper
2 Tbsp balsamic vinegar
4 x 160g [5½oz] cod fillets
400g [14oz] cavolo nero,
    coarse stalks removed
1 Tbsp olive oil
3 Tbsp water

For the hollandaise
175g [¾ cup] unsalted butter
3 egg yolks
3 Tbsp water
juice of ½ lemon, plus more to taste

Preheat the oven to 110°C/225°F/Gas ¼.

For the beetroot and cod, peel the beetroot and boil for 30 minutes in lightly salted water, then drain and cut into very thin slices. Place them in roasting pans lined with baking parchment. Brush with the balsamic vinegar and bake in the oven for 1 hour. They will be dehydrated and pleasantly chewy, but not crisp.

Get the ingredients ready for the hollandaise. Melt the butter, discard any froth on top and let it cool to lukewarm. Get a saucepan and a heatproof mixing bowl that will sit stably over the pan. Half-fill the pan with water and bring to a simmer. Reduce the heat as low as it can go while still keeping the water simmering. Place the egg yolks in the heatproof mixing bowl and place over the pan of simmering water. (It's important that the pan is over a low heat, or the eggs will scramble.) Using a balloon whisk, start beating the eggs, then whisk in the water for about 3 minutes until it is pale yellow. Keep whisking, then start adding the melted butter, drizzling it in, whisking all the time, until it is all incorporated. You should have a lovely smooth, thick sauce. Season with lemon juice, salt and pepper.

Meanwhile, place the cod fillets in a dish, sprinkle with salt and pepper, cover with clingfilm [plastic wrap] and leave to rest in the refrigerator until ready to cook. Rinse the cavolo nero, drain well and chop roughly, then sauté it in the olive oil for 3–4 minutes and season to taste with salt and pepper.

Place the cod in a sauté pan, add the water, cover with a lid and steam for 3–5 minutes. To check if it's done, slightly push the fish with your thumb: it should feel firm, but with a slight softness.

Serve the cod with the hollandaise, dehydrated beetroot and cavolo nero.

Pork chops with Brussels sprouts

Pork chops are an everyday food in Denmark. In Copenhagen restaurants you see a lot of pork on the menu; restaurants like to emphasize the quality of the meat and which farm it is from.

Serves 4

400g [14oz] Brussels sprouts
4 eating apples
4 big juicy pork chops
100g [7 Tbsp] salted butter
sea salt and freshly ground
    black pepper
3 dill sprigs, chopped

Rinse the Brussels sprouts and remove and reserve the outer leaves. Cut the sprouts into quarters. Core the apples and cut them into wedges.

Fry the pork chops in a frying pan with half the butter for 2–3 minutes on each side, or until cooked through, sprinkling with salt and pepper. Remove from the pan and keep them warm in a low oven.

In the same frying pan, melt the remaining butter and sauté the apples and Brussels sprouts for 5–6 minutes, again sprinkling with salt and pepper. For the last couple of minutes, add the leaves.

Cut the pork chops into thick slices and serve with the apples, sprouts and browned butter, adding the dill.

Above and opposite: Nyboder, an area full of naval
barracks, some of which date back to the 1600s. They
were built by Christian IV who had a huge influence on
Copenhagen, both then and now. The living quarters come
in different sizes, they are quirky, and they boast both
history and charm. A lot of my school friends grew up here.

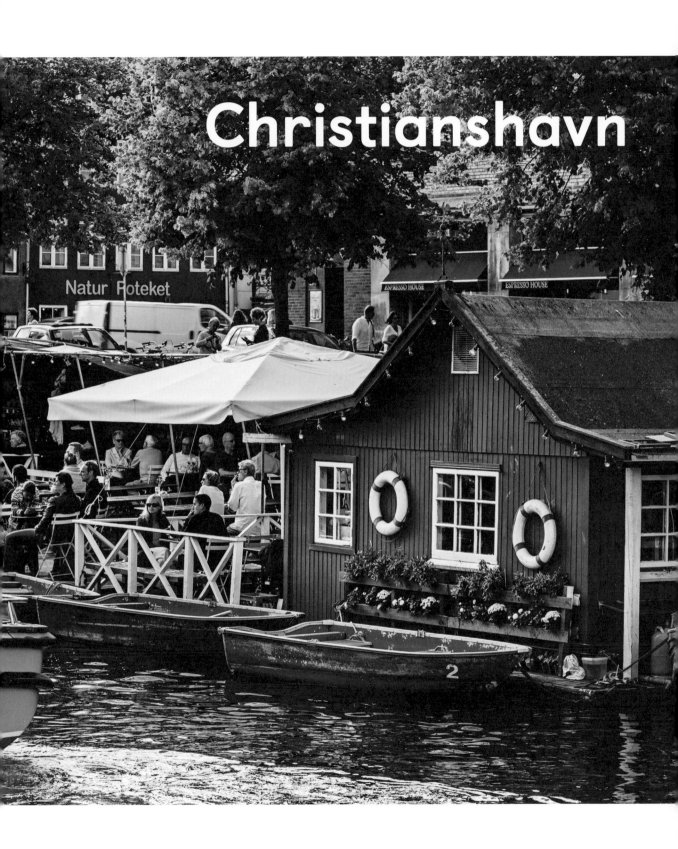

Christianshavn

Christianshavn, destination for the noma pilgrims who flock to Copenhagen, is a relatively small but charming area across the harbour from Gammelholm, on a system of canals. There are a lot of private yachts, both big and small, moored along the quay as they would be in a marina, and many houseboats, too. It's a very old part of Copenhagen and most of the buildings are 300–400 years old. Vilhelm Hammershøi, the famous Danish painter, lived here a hundred years ago.

Now it has been gentrified, but thankfully not entirely so. Many quaint courtyards remain, along with outdoor areas along the canals. For a short time, when I was about six years old, I lived in a small commune in one of the old townhouses in **Wildersgade**. It was a fun time.

In Wildersgade, there are two well-known pubs: **Eiffel Bar** and **Fingerbøllet**. My brother is named after one of the regulars at Eiffel Bar. As a child, I would go to use the bathroom at Fingerbøllet late at night. I was scared to use the bathroom in our backyard, as I was afraid of the dark. Fingerbøllet was much nicer; sometimes I would stay and talk to the barmaid and she would give me an orange soda before I went back to bed. I really liked my little late-night outings.

Danes love marzipan, both as an ingredient in their cakes and just as an iconic bar covered with dark chocolate. These were my favourite chocolate bars as a kid. When I was around six years old, I didn't really like school, and the school bus stop was a bit far away from my home in Christianshavn. So I often managed to convince the grown-ups that I could do something else. With my sister Silla, we would accompany one of the adults in our commune to his workshop close by, where he was building a boat. Those were fun days. We didn't eat lunch, but we had a lot of marzipan chocolate bars and sodas!

This was a district with a strong identity. People knew each other and would keep an eye out for each other. It was not posh. There were many small apartments with no central heating and most houses had the toilet in the backyard. The neighbourhood has gone through a huge transformation, the houses are now renovated and the area has dozens of cafés and restaurants.

Ravelinen, an iconic restaurant on Christianshavn Vold facing the lake, serves classic Danish food both for lunch and dinner. For really good Italian food, **Era Ora** at Christianshavn Kanal is an all-time classic in Copenhagen; they have held a Michelin star for more than 20 years.

These days, Christianshavn connects to the city centre by means of the bicycle and pedestrian bridge over to Nyhavn (page 34). From the bridge, you are welcomed into Christianshavn with the **Copenhagen Street Food market** where you will find salads, burgers, Korean food and ice cream, wine and beer. It is the perfect place to hang out during the summer, as it's great for picnics on the quayside, watching the boats. Copenhagen gets a special buzz as soon as the weather turns fine: people flock outdoors and you'll find folk everywhere, hoping to get a bit of sun on their face and a breeze in their hair.

The famous chocolate marzipan bar

When I was a child, I would hang out where the boats were built.
Often, the grown-ups would give us fizzy drinks, or marzipan
chocolate bars from Anthon Berg, wrapped up in pink paper.

Makes about 12

For the marzipan
350g [2¾ cups] blanched almonds
100g [¾ cup] icing [confectioner's]
   sugar, plus more to dust
50ml [3½ Tbsp] water

To finish the bars
200g [7oz] tempered dark
   [bittersweet] chocolate,
   60% cocoa solids (page 21)

For the marzipan, whizz the blanched almonds in a food processor and keep whizzing until they become a paste. Add the icing sugar, whizz again, then add the water and whizz again. Take the marzipan out of the food processor and knead it on a work surface dusted with icing sugar. Form it into a big brick-like shape and leave to rest in refrigerator for 2 hours or overnight.

To finish the bars, cut the marzipan into 12 even-sized rectangular bars while you temper the chocolate (page 21). Dip each bar in the tempered chocolate, making sure they are covered, then place on a wire rack until the chocolate has set.

Lagkagehuset

Another iconic venue in Christianshavn is the bakery **Lagkagehuset**, which has these days evolved into the bakery chain **Ole & Steen** and been rolled out everywhere. The first bakery, owned by Ole, was located in the centre of Christianshavn and the original name came from the 1930s building in which it was housed. The building's structure resembles a layer cake, which in Danish is 'lagkage'.

In the 1990s, I would bicycle out there on Sunday mornings to buy bread, Danish pastries and *kanelstang*, as they had hands-down the best quality around. Ole, the owner of that first bakery, set in motion a new bakery culture in Copenhagen a full 10 years before hipster bearded bakers and their sourdough became a worldwide religion. Back then, Ole just baked better-tasting bread.

Now there are a slew of independent bakeries, all doing their own thing, but together renewing the tradition of baking in Copenhagen and working with local grains and flour. There have always been a lot of bakeries in the city, which open early in the morning in good time for the citizens to buy their fresh bread and pastries.

Right: The original Lagkagehuset on Torvegade

Cinnamon kringle (Kanelstang)

A classic soft sweet bread and my personal favourite, found in all bakeries around Copenhagen. You can eat it all day long.

Serves 8

For the dough

50g [2oz] fresh yeast

500ml [2 cups] lukewarm milk

1 egg, lightly beaten, plus 1 more

850g [6⅓ cups] plain [all-purpose] flour, plus more to dust

100g [½ cup] caster [granulated] sugar

1 tsp ground cardamom

½ tsp fine sea salt

150g [⅔ cup] softened salted butter, cubed

50g [⅓ cup] almonds, finely chopped

icing [confectioner's] sugar, to dust

For the filling

200g [¾ cup plus 2 Tbsp] softened unsalted butter

150g [¾ cup] soft brown sugar

2 Tbsp ground cinnamon

For the dough, crumble the yeast into the milk and stir to dissolve, then add the beaten egg. Now, in a separate bowl, mix the flour, sugar, cardamom and salt. Rub the butter into the flour mixture with your hands, then mix in the milk mixture. Knead well on a floured surface. Put the dough into a bowl, cover with a tea towel and let it rise for 1–2 hours, or until doubled in size.

For the filling, mix together the butter, brown sugar and cinnamon. Divide the dough in half and roll each piece out on a floured surface to make a rectangle measuring about 45 x 30cm [18 x 12in]. Spread the cinnamon filling in the middle of each piece, leaving 2cm [¾in] clear along the short sides and 5cm [2in] clear along the long sides. Fold the 2cm [¾in] ends in over the filling at the ends. Fold one long side over towards the middle, then fold the other long side over, too, so that there is a slight overlap and the filling is completely encased.

Line 2 baking sheets with baking parchment and place a pastry piece on each. Cover with a tea towel and leave to rise for 30 minutes.

Preheat the oven to 180°C/350°F/Gas 4. Lightly beat the remaining egg and use it to brush the pastries. Sprinkle the chopped almonds on top. Bake for 18–20 minutes. Leave to cool on a wire rack for 10 minutes, then cut into slices and dust with icing sugar to serve.

Christiania

This community – a self-proclaimed autonomous district of **Christianshavn** – is one of Copenhagen's top tourist attractions. An abandoned military area, it was occupied by squatters in the spirit of the 1968 hippie movement, and was an attempt to build an alternative, parallel, self-sufficient society with its own VAT system and flag and a more equitable way of living. The creators of Christiania belonged to a movement that challenged the establishment, thought deeply about women's rights and craved more equality, more democratic housing and more space for those who didn't fit into society's norms.

Did Christiania succeed in keeping up the original utopian ideals? Probably not (and who could?), but they are now fighting for their right to exist.

For us as kids, Christiania was an enormous playground and the benign neglect of our parents meant there was even more freedom!

Since those childhood days, I have continued to visit Christiania all my life. I go there for concerts, to see friends, have coffee, hang out at the canal and visit the **Christmas Market**. I like to walk in from the back and avoid Pusher Street (you can guess from the name what that street is famous for). Instead, I like to go for walks on the embankment and to eat at **Morgenstedet**. I like their organic, vegetarian approach to cooking. Though the food is about as far from the noma effect as you can imagine – it's a very old-school approach, almost like time-travelling to my 1970s childhood – it is fresh, tastes good and you always feel wholesome after eating their soup and salad.

When I was a young girl, my mum and I ate one night at **Spiseloppen**, a restaurant in Christiania that was a big hit in the 1980s. We had **Fru Eckersberg** cake for dessert and it was so good that we took a piece of the cake with us for my stepdad to eat at home. We went to a lot of bars after the restaurant and carried the cake with us all night, but unfortunately my mother finally lost it accidentally when going home over Knippelsbro, the bridge connecting Christianshavn with central Copenhagen.

Mr Eckersberg was an important artist of Danish culture's Golden Age, during the first half of the 19th century. Painters such as Eckersberg, Købke and Lundby, writers such as Hans Christian Andersen and Søren Kierkegaard, and other significant artists not widely known outside Denmark all date from this period. They were inspired by German and English Romanticism, and paintings from the period can be seen at **Thorvaldsen's Museum** (next to Christiansborg). Anyway, maybe Fru – which means 'Mrs' in Danish – Eckersberg made this cake for Mr Eckersberg? If so, lucky him!

Opposite: The Christmas Market on Bådsmandsstræde, Christiania

Salad and soup

When I was growing up, in the 1970s, this sort of thing was called hippie food because it was green or contained (gasp!) spices. There were a few places that served hippie food in Copenhagen, Morgenstedet in Christiania being among them. I like their way of cooking – it's no fuss and very honest.

Both recipes serve 4

Celery and orange salad

600g [1lb 5oz] celeriac
[celery root]
2 oranges
50g [½ cup] hazelnuts
50ml [3½ Tbsp] orange juice
2 Tbsp hazelnut oil
6 Tbsp finely chopped mint
sea salt and freshly ground
black pepper

Spinach chickpea soup

300g [1½ cups] dried chickpeas
[garbanzo beans]
1 Tbsp grapeseed oil
2 garlic cloves, finely chopped
1 onion, chopped
2–3 Tbsp garam masala
1 green chilli
75g [2½oz] fresh root ginger,
finely grated
200g [7oz] courgettes [zucchini],
halved lengthways, then sliced
2 litres [8½ cups] vegetable stock
sea salt and freshly ground
black pepper
500g [1lb 2oz] spinach, well rinsed
juice of ½ lemon

Celery and orange salad

Peel and grate or shred the celeriac. Peel the oranges and cut into slices. Place both in a big mixing bowl.

Toast the hazelnuts in a dry frying pan for about 3–4 minutes, then leave to cool. Chop roughly and add to the salad.

Mix in the orange juice, hazelnut oil and mint, then season to taste with salt and pepper.

Spinach chickpea soup

Soak the chickpeas in plenty of cold water overnight. The next day, drain and put them in a large saucepan, cover with fresh water and bring to the boil over a medium heat. Boil for 30 minutes, then drain and leave for later.

In a separate large saucepan, heat the oil over a medium heat and sauté the garlic, onion, garam masala, chilli and ginger for 3–4 minutes. Add the courgettes, mix well and sauté for 2–3 minutes, making sure the vegetables do not catch on the pan.

Pour in the vegetable stock and bring to the boil, then reduce the heat and simmer for 5 minutes. Now add the drained chickpeas and simmer for another 5 minutes. Season to taste with salt and pepper, add the spinach and let it simmer for 2 minutes. Season with lemon juice. Serve with the salad.

Fru Eckersberg cake

A classic cake that everybody seems to have forgotten. Eckersberg was a famous painter of the Danish Golden Age. I have never been able to find out if the cake has anything to do with him (probably not), but it is outstanding!

Serves 8–10

unsalted butter, for the tin

For the almond macaroon
300g [2½ cups] blanched almonds
300g [2 cups plus 2 Tbsp] icing [confectioner's] sugar
6 egg whites

For the mocha cream
150g [⅔ cup] softened unsalted butter
75g [½ cup] icing [confectioner's] sugar
75g [2½oz] dark [bittersweet] chocolate, 60–65% cocoa solids, finely chopped
50ml [3½ Tbsp] very hot, extra-strong coffee
1 egg yolk

Preheat the oven to 160°C/325°F/Gas 3. Line the base of a 24cm [9½in] diameter springform cake tin with baking parchment and butter it lightly.

For the almond macaroon, grind the nuts in a food processor until they are finely chopped. Transfer to a bowl and sift in the icing sugar, blending well. In a separate bowl, whisk the egg whites until stiff, then fold in the nut mixture. Pour the mixture into the prepared tin and bake for 50–60 minutes. Remove from the oven and leave the cake, still on its baking parchment, on a wire rack for 15 minutes, then peel off the parchment and let the cake cool completely.

For the mocha cream, beat the butter and icing sugar together until pale and fluffy. Put the chopped chocolate in a jug, pour over the very hot coffee and leave until the chocolate has melted, stirring occasionally. When the chocolate has completely melted, stir in the egg yolk. Add the chocolate mixture to the butter mixture and mix it well.

Carefully – it is very fragile! – place the cake on a serving dish. Spread the mocha cream evenly over the cake using a palette knife. Refrigerate the cake until ready to serve.

Holmen

This area to the north-east of Christianshavn is home to **Amass**, Matt Orlando's great restaurant that is doing cutting-edge work on sustainability. It is located in a part of Copenhagen that used to be sealed off by the Danish Navy for military purposes only, but is now an open, up-and-coming area with tons of dynamism.

Amass is a restaurant that other chefs around the world aspire to keep up with. They have an enlightened waste programme that constantly questions how to run a restaurant with zero waste. The food they serve tells a story about terroir, it is organic and shows what is possible even when you refuse to compromise on a strict sustainable ideology. I highly recommend eating there, both for the wonderful food (of course) and also for the inspiring journey the restaurant is on. Even if that doesn't do it for you, their potato bread alone makes it worth a visit…

You can either bicycle out to Amass across the bridge at the end of Nyhavn and through the Architect School located at Holmen, or take a yellow public transport boat that leaves from Nyhavn and other stops in Copenhagen Harbour.

There is a lot to explore at Holmen where you can find wild and untamed landscape within the city limits of Copenhagen. If you are interested in wild food, get the **Byhøst** and the **Vild Mad App**, then go out and explore and find all the great things that grow around there. Always, though, be gentle and respect nature.

Left: Amass Restaurant
Opposite: Holmen

The great transformation

Something seismic happened in Copenhagen in 2003: **noma** opened.

It wasn't an international success right away and many Copenhageners were sceptical. Chefs in Copenhagen criticized the food and questioned serving (for dessert) *øllebrød*, the Danish rye bread porridge that is a classic poor man's food (see page 224 for my recipe).

I have eaten at noma almost every year since it opened and have personally experienced the journey that chef René Redzepi and his team have undertaken. I have eaten outstanding meals there and I will never forget some of my favourite dishes from the early days. They have inspired me and led me to a deeper understanding of where I come from. Food and eating are not just about taste – they are also about memory, about one's own story. So many smells and tastes bring on specific sensations that lead directly to your own conscious or subconscious food memories.

In about 2004, I had dinner at noma with my sister Silla, who is also a chef. She's not a very sentimental person; she never talks about the past and definitely doesn't dwell on it… that is more my territory! That evening, we ate snacks with chicken skin, lumpfish roe, smoked cheese and beef tartare served with tarragon cream. It set us both off down a road into the past. She spoke about our *mormor* and the beach house where we spent the Danish summers as children, and about all the things she would cook for us. We had a wonderful evening together and neither of us will ever forget how the food brought out a side of my sister I rarely see. I still dream of that tarragon emulsion and chicken skin snack; they are locked into my personal food memory bank.

Now the original noma is history, the new noma has opened and René and his team are on a fresh adventure. The new location was formerly a derelict building, and it is on the border of Christiania (page 88) – I went to some wild parties there, way back. The whole project is mind-boggling and the meal I had there was interesting, advanced and an exploration of terroir and flavour.

Noma has changed Copenhagen, perhaps forever. When the globe discovered noma and it was crowned the world's best restaurant, people flew to Denmark just to eat there. It was the noma effect. Restaurants began to open up all over town, either run by noma alumni, or by other people who saw the way that food in Copenhagen was evolving.

Before noma, Danes never had a strong restaurant culture. We have always had a strong *food* culture, but that has mostly gone on at home, and often seemed overshadowed by that of France or Italy. All that is history now. The understanding of the Nordic terroir, seasons and lifestyle has deepened, been re-interpreted and then its own language created. Some of the more outlandish restaurant dishes may seem a world away from traditional Danish food culture, but there is a clear link to its history.

The noma family now has two new outlets. The first is **108**, which also has a café where I often take coffee. The food here is casual but still a bit experimental. I have had milk skin topped with vegetables, and some amazing desserts with blackcurrants (I love blackcurrants). And then there's **BARR**, which is casual Danish food made with the very best local ingredients – which is exactly what I love! It's a great place to eat dinner at the bar.

Clockwise from top: Christianshavn canal; BARR; 108

Schnitzel with anchovies, horseradish and capers

Danish schnitzel is made from pork and classically served with brown butter, horseradish, capers and anchovies. I think a dash of lemon serves it well.

Serves 4

50g [⅓ cup] plain [all-purpose] flour
sea salt and freshly ground black pepper
2 medium eggs
100g [1¼ cups] breadcrumbs
4 x 150g [5½oz] pork loin schnitzels
400g [14oz] Brussels sprouts
65g [¼ cup] salted butter
4 Tbsp capers, drained and rinsed
4 canned anchovy fillets, chopped
4 Tbsp finely grated horseradish, ideally fresh rather than from a jar
handful of dill sprigs
2 lemons, cut in half

Mix the flour with salt and pepper on a plate. On a second plate, lightly beat the eggs; on a third plate, spread out the breadcrumbs.

Roll the meat in the seasoned flour, making sure it is thoroughly coated, then dip each piece into the egg until coated. Drain off the excess egg and turn the schnitzels in the crumbs until completely coated.

Trim the sprouts and cut them into quarters. Heat 20g [1½ Tbsp] of the butter in a frying pan and sauté the sprouts for 5 minutes, adding a few spoons of water if they start to stick to the pan and burn. Remove from the heat and keep warm.

Meanwhile, melt 30g [2 Tbsp] more of the butter in a large frying pan until bubbling briskly. Fry the schnitzels for 2–3 minutes on each side until golden and crisp. Place them on a plate.

Wipe the pan and heat the remaining butter until golden, then fry the capers and anchovies over a high heat for a few minutes.

Serve each schnitzel with the horseradish and dill on top, sprinkled with the fried capers, anchovies and brown butter and accompanied by the lemon halves and sauteed sprouts.

Baked cauliflower with garlicky kale and walnuts

I grew up with 'masked cauliflower', which is cauliflower boiled to near-death, then covered in a white sauce and served with prawns. It was not my favourite! However, I love cauliflower, so here is my modern version.

Serves 4

1 whole cauliflower
2 Tbsp softened salted butter
sea salt and freshly ground
　　black pepper
300g [10½oz] kale
1 Tbsp olive oil
100g [1 cup] walnuts, chopped
2 garlic cloves, finely chopped

Preheat the oven to 180°C/350°F/Gas 4 and line a baking sheet with baking parchment.

Place the cauliflower on the baking sheet, spread with the butter and sprinkle with pepper. Bake for 1 hour, now and then basting with the butter.

Meanwhile, rinse the kale several times in cold water in a large bowl until there is no more dirt in the bowl. Remove the leaves from the stalks (discard the stalks), squeeze out the water, then chop the leaves.

Heat the oil in a large frying pan and sauté the walnuts and garlic for a few minutes. Add the kale and sauté for a further 5 minutes. Season to taste with salt and pepper and serve on top of the baked cauliflower.

Islands Brygge

Islands Brygge, a former quay where large freighters were once moored, is a real Copenhagen destination during the summer. When the sun is out, Islands Brygge swarms with young people and families, both in the park facing the waterfront and the public swimming pool in the harbour, which has a sauna connected to it for the Nordic winter swimmers. The water is clean and you can swim in the harbour all year round. Boats are on the water and people sunbathe, swim and drink beer, serenaded by bands in the streets.

It is unique to have spaces like this in the centre of a city and to be able to swim in the harbour. During your visit, I recommend a walk along the quay down to the pedestrian-bicycling bridge called **Bryggebroen** (pictured on pages 104–105). Or why not bicycle across the ramp over the harbour to Vesterbro (page 183), then cycle through Vesterbro along the lakes and through Østerbro (page 231) down to The Little Mermaid? You will then have bicycled almost a full circle around the boroughs of central Copenhagen, which has only been possible in the last five years and proves just how accessible the city has become.

The neighbourhood around here has seen a gentrification of significant proportions. As a child I would visit here because I went to school with kids who lived in the area. All the flats facing the waterfront have lots of daylight and are grand, with big windows and high ceilings. When you turn into the side streets, you can see that this was once a working-class community, full of one- or two-bedroom flats, now invaded by young people and all kinds of hipsters. Even the **former factories** are now fancy apartments with waterfront views.

Tobi's Café

You'll find this place in Leifsgade, about 500 metres from the waterfront. Here, they serve coffee and tea in Royal Copenhagen cups (a particular weakness of mine, see page 151). They put on a nice breakfast, it is a good place to take tea and cake (especially their carrot cake) or a light supper and you can also get a Copenhagen café burger. A really great spot for locals and for all the rest of us who want to get lost at Islands Brygge.

Ismageriet ice cream

A bit further out from Islands Brygge towards where TV-Byen (the Danish Broadcasting Corporation) is located, you'll find Ismageriet, which means 'dairy shop'. They make Italian-style gelato with organic milk. It's fun and the selection is great, even if the interior is a bit old-school. Most Danes think the good ice cream is worth a five-mile bike ride!

Wulff & Konstali

An excellent food shop offering breakfast, lunch and dinner, both to eat in and take away. They also have coffee and cake. So it's ideal to go there, buy food for picnic, then go down to the harbour and relax and have a swim in the outdoor pool area.

Opposite: Tobi's Café

Central Copenhagen

The centre of Copenhagen is known for its spires and charm. It has many parks and squares, small quirky streets and enough atmosphere to make you want to keep on exploring, even when you know the city well. There are distinctly different areas with a mix of architecture from the 16th century onwards, and a wide range of places to drink, grab some street food, or relax over a more elaborate dinner. You get a feel for the city quickly because it is not too big, but has enough going on for it to feel cosmopolitan. It's easy to get around either on foot or by bike.

I love the more remote part of the centre around Christiansborg riding stables; it is beautiful all year round and the stables are open to the public. Also around here is the **National Museum** which has a great display on Danish history, not least the Vikings; even just the buildings are worth a visit. **Thorvaldsens Museum** is close by, between the canals and Christansborg. It showcases the Golden Age in pictures and sculptures. A short walk away is **K-Bar**, one of the first venues in Copenhagen to really take cocktail-making seriously. The outdoor space is lovely in the summer, as is the one at **Ved Stranden**. This is just like an old shop in the city centre. You walk in and then go through into the back rooms. It is *hyggelig* and, most importantly, it has a good selection of wines, including some great Austrian wines.

After living with my family in London, Paris and Washington DC, we returned to Copenhagen in the mid-1990s. We bought our first home on Åbenrå street – a small apartment right in the centre of the old town. It was charming, with French doors opening on to a tiny courtyard, and a galley kitchen that I lined with shelves for my equipment and cookbooks.

What it lacked in space, it made up for in spirit. I loved cooking in that kitchen, even though every time I bought a new piece of kit I had to rearrange the whole room. I cooked, I baked, I entertained, I wrote recipes. I cooked spaghetti carbonara – my children's favourite at the time – vegetable patties, salads and fishcakes, dream cakes and pancakes and often, when I entertained, roast lamb. Cooking in that room coincided with my early days as a chef. I loved creating new ideas in my kitchen; I would sit on my stool surrounded by chopping boards and simmering pots, trying to keep track of my new venture: a catering company.

In the city centre, **Storkespringvandet**, the fountain, is a key meeting point. When I was a teenager, it was a place where I would hang out with friends in the summer on rollerskates or skateboards. I never skated myself but spent a lot of time admiring the boys who did! There were no cafés back then, or even designer shops. At that time in the early 1980s, things didn't seem prosperous. We were told there were no jobs, no future – but at the same time new places were opening and the yuppie culture hit new parts of town. We learned fast how to drink cappuccino and change identity according to which part of town we were in.

Then, in 1989, **Café Europa** opened on this spot. It is one of very few places that I've been visiting since it started. It is in a great location, it opens early, the coffee is good, and the food maintains a high standard. It is expensive, but that is to be expected in this part of town. I sometimes go for breakfast or lunch and always have a salad, or *smørrebrød*. If you want to treat yourself, their pastries are really good, too.

This is the main shopping area. Visit **Porcelænskælderne** for an amazing collection of Royal Copenhagen: it's a favourite spot of mine. But you might spend too much money…

Pages 106–107: Christiansborg
Opposite: Magstrade

Poppy seed pastries (Tebirkes)

My favourite Danish pastry to eat for breakfast. In Copenhagen it is called a *tebirkes*, though other parts of Denmark refer to it as *københaverne*.

Makes 20

150g [5½oz] marzipan, at least 60% almonds, coarsely grated (see page 82 for homemade)
125g [½ cup plus 1 Tbsp] softened salted butter
3 Tbsp caster [granulated] sugar
1 medium egg, lightly beaten, to glaze
50–100g [⅓–⅔ cup] poppy seeds

For the pastry dough
25g [1oz] fresh yeast
150ml [⅔ cup] lukewarm water
1 medium egg, lightly beaten
½ tsp fine sea salt
1 Tbsp caster [granulated] sugar
325g [scant 2½ cups] plain [all-purpose] flour, plus more to dust
300g [1⅓ cups] cold unsalted butter, in thin slices

First, make the pastry dough. Crumble the yeast into the lukewarm water, then add the egg, salt and sugar. Stir in the flour, then knead on a floured surface until smooth and elastic. Put in a bowl, cover with clingfilm [plastic wrap] and refrigerate for 15 minutes. When ready, roll out the dough on a floured surface into a 45cm [18in] square. Arrange a square of the butter slices in the centre at a 45° angle to the corners of the dough so it forms a diamond inside the square. Fold the dough corners over the butter to encase it fully and seal the joins well. Roll out the dough into a rectangle. Make sure it doesn't crack and expose the butter.

Now take a shorter side and fold one-third of the rectangle over towards the centre. Do the same with the opposite side. You will now have a pile of 3 layers, as you would with a business letter. Wrap in clingfilm and refrigerate for 15 minutes. Repeat this rolling and folding procedure 3 times in total, letting the dough rest for 15 minutes in the refrigerator between each.

For the filling, mix the marzipan, butter and sugar into a smooth paste and set aside at room temperature.

Roll out the dough on a lightly floured surface to 56 x 36cm [22 x 14in], then cut it in half lengthways. Spread half the filling evenly, lengthways, down the centre of a dough rectangle. Fold the plain sides of dough over the filling. Repeat with the other dough rectangle and the rest of the filling. Push the seams of both parcels gently together and turn them over so that they are seam side down. Brush with the egg and dredge with poppy seeds. Cut across into 5cm [2in] slices and place on baking sheets lined with baking parchment. Cover with tea towels and leave in a warm place for 30 minutes. Preheat the oven to 220°C/425°F/Gas 7.

Bake for 5 minutes, then reduce the oven temperature to 200°C/400°F/Gas 6 and bake for 15 minutes.

My favourite breakfast

When you go to a café, you tend to get a lot of brunch all on one plate. I'm really not a fan of that kind of service. I prefer it when items are presented separately, as they do at Café Europa, so that is always a safe choice when I go out for breakfast.

Serves 4

500g [1lb 2oz] spinach
2 tomatoes
8 medium eggs
50ml [3½ Tbsp] whole milk
½ nutmeg, freshly grated
½ tsp chilli flakes
sea salt and freshly ground
   black pepper
2 Tbsp olive oil
1 Tbsp salted butter
4 slices of bread
10 slices of Parma ham

Rinse the spinach in cold water until the water runs clean, then drain it well. Slice the tomatoes, then scoop out and discard their seeds.

Beat the eggs well in a mixing bowl, adding the milk, nutmeg, chilli flakes and salt and pepper.

Heat the oil in a frying pan over a medium-high heat, then sauté the tomatoes for 2 minutes. Add the spinach and sauté for 1 minute more, then pour in the egg mixture and fold gently until the eggs have set.

Meanwhile, melt the butter in another frying pan. Fry the bread in the butter on both sides.

Serve the warm bread and eggs with the Parma ham on the side.

Liver pâté (Leverpostej)

This paté is probably the most-eaten topping on rye bread in the whole of Denmark. I bet you 70% of all Danes have *leverpostej* in their refrigerator.

Serves 6–8

For the pickled beetroot
500g [1lb 2oz] beetroot [beet]
sea salt
400ml [1¾ cups] apple cider vinegar
300g [1½ cups] granulated sugar
1 cinnamon stick
2 bay leaves
6 cloves
4 cardamom pods
1 tsp black peppercorns

For the pâté
5–6 canned anchovy fillets
40g [3 Tbsp] salted butter, plus more for the mould and to serve
40g [¼ cup] plain [all-purpose] flour
450ml [scant 2 cups] half-fat milk
1 large onion, grated
2 tsp sea salt
1½ tsp freshly ground black pepper
¼ tsp freshly grated nutmeg
1 tsp ground allspice
1 tsp ground cloves
225g [½lb] minced [ground] pork back fat
500g [1lb 2oz] minced [ground] pig's liver
2 small eggs, lightly beaten
3 bay leaves

For the mushrooms
200g [7oz] Portobello mushrooms
80g [⅓ cup] salted butter
1 Tbsp olive oil
3 sprigs of thyme

Start with the pickled beetroot. Boil the beetroots with their skins on in salted water for about 30 minutes, depending on their size. Check if they are tender by piercing with a small knife.

Meanwhile, make the brine: add all the remaining beetroot ingredients to a saucepan, bring to the boil, stirring to dissolve the sugar, then reduce the heat and simmer for 5 minutes. Remove from the heat and leave to cool.

When the beetroots are tender, rinse them in cold water and remove the skins. Cut into wedges or slices and place in a sterilized 1-litre [1-quart] glass jar (page 56). Pour the brine over, seal the jar and place in a dark cupboard at room temperature for 2–3 weeks.

For the pâté, mash the anchovies until they become a lumpy paste. Melt the butter in a heavy-based saucepan, add the flour and mix to form a roux. Little by little, add the milk, stirring constantly. Bring to the boil and stir in the mashed anchovies, the onion, salt, pepper, nutmeg, allspice and cloves. Add the fat to the boiling sauce, stirring constantly until it melts. Add the liver and stir until evenly distributed. Remove the pan from the heat and cool slightly.

Preheat the oven to 180°C/350°F/Gas 4.

Add the eggs to the pâté and stir well, then pour the mixture into a buttered terrine mould, placing the bay leaves on top. Put the mould into a roasting pan. Pour hot water from the kettle into the roasting pan to come halfway up the sides of the mould. Carefully slide into the oven and bake, uncovered, for 1 hour 15 minutes. Leave to cool for about 15 minutes.

Meanwhile, slice the mushrooms. Melt the butter in a frying pan, add the oil and sauté the mushrooms for 4 minutes, seasoning with salt and pepper. Serve the pâté with the mushrooms and pickled beetroot, as well as slices of toasted rye bread.

Roast pork buns with red cabbage and cucumber salad

Pork sandwiches with red cabbage is a classic. If you want the authentic experience in Copenhagen, eat it at Isted Grill in Istedgade, a real Danish grill-bar, from a world pre-dating large fast-food chains.

Makes 4

For the cucumber salad
200ml [¾ cup] apple cider vinegar
100ml [⅓ cup] water
100g [½ cup] caster [granulated]
　sugar
sea salt and freshly ground
　black pepper
1 cucumber

For the red cabbage
200g [7oz] red cabbage, cored
　and shredded
1 Tbsp coarse sea salt
1 large cooking apple, such as
　Bramley, peeled, cored and
　finely chopped
2 Tbsp apple cider vinegar
3 Tbsp extra virgin olive oil
1 tsp caster [granulated] sugar

For the buns
12 x 2cm [¾in] thick slices of lean
　pork belly with rind
4 focaccia buns

Preheat the oven to 200°C/400°F/Gas 6.

Start with the cucumber salad. Mix the vinegar and water in a non-reactive bowl and add the sugar, salt and pepper. Stir until the sugar has dissolved. Cut the cucumber into very thin slices and add to the vinegar mixture. Leave to stand for at least 30 minutes.

For the red cabbage, put the cabbage in a bowl and mix well with the salt. Set aside for 15 minutes.

Sprinkle the pork belly slices with salt and pepper. Line a roasting pan with baking parchment and put a trivet on the parchment. Lay the pork slices on the trivet and roast for 20 minutes, or until crisp, turning over once.

Now return to the red cabbage. Squeeze the cabbage and carefully rinse in cold water. Drain well and mix with the apple. Whisk the vinegar, oil and sugar together with some seasoning until the sugar and salt have dissolved, then fold this into the cabbage mixture.

Cut the focaccia buns in half. Spread some cabbage on the bases, place 2–3 slices of roast pork on each, then top with the cucumber salad and the top halves of the buns. Serve right away.

Frikadeller

All countries around the world have a meatball. This is ours, made from pork and veal. The slang term for this is 'deller', and you can find veggie 'deller' or fish 'deller', too. Cooked regularly in most households, a true Danish classic, everyday food.

Serves 4

For the barley
100g [½ cup] pearl barley
sea salt and freshly ground
    black pepper
1 preserved lemon
leaves from a small bunch of
    flat-leaf parsley, chopped
handful of chervil sprigs

For the meatballs
250g [9oz] minced [ground] beef
250g [9oz] minced [ground] pork
1 onion, finely chopped
2 Tbsp thyme leaves
2 medium eggs, lightly beaten
3 Tbsp breadcrumbs
2 Tbsp plain [all-purpose] flour
100ml [⅓ cup] whole milk
1–2 Tbsp extra virgin olive oil
1–3 Tbsp salted butter

For the cabbage and béchamel
1 large Hispi cabbage
50g [3½ Tbsp] salted butter
50g [6 Tbsp] plain [all-purpose]
    flour
300ml [1¼ cups] whole milk
¼–½ tsp freshly grated nutmeg

For the barley, cook the pearl barley in boiling, lightly salted water for 20 minutes, then drain. Rinse the preserved lemon, then finely chop it. Mix the barley, preserved lemon and parsley together in a bowl.

For the meatballs, mix the meats with 1–2 tsp sea salt and some pepper using your hands. Add the onion, thyme and eggs, and beat well. Stir in the breadcrumbs and flour and beat again. Lastly, mix in the milk.

Preheat the oven to 180°C/350°F/Gas 4.

Use a spoon and a hand to shape the meatball mixture into small, round balls. Heat the olive oil and butter together in a large frying pan, add the meatballs and fry on all sides until golden brown. Transfer to an ovenproof dish and finish cooking in the oven for 10 minutes.

Meanwhile, for the cabbage and béchamel, quarter the cabbage, remove the core and shred the leaves. Bring lightly salted water to the boil in a saucepan and add the cabbage. Return to the boil and let it cook for 4 minutes. Drain, saving 200ml [¾ cup] of the cooking liquid.

For the béchamel sauce, melt the butter in a heavy-based saucepan. Whisk in the flour and cook until foaming, about 1 minute. Little by little add the reserved cabbage cooking liquid, then the milk, whisking constantly until boiling. Add the cabbage and return to the boil, then season to taste with the nutmeg, salt and pepper and leave to simmer for 2 minutes.

Serve the meatballs with the cabbage and béchamel sauce and barley, garnished with the chervil.

Roast lamb with tarragon, mint and parsley

I love lamb, though it can be difficult to find on menus in Copenhagen.
I cook it often, with seasonal herbs.

Serves 8

1 leg of lamb, about 3kg [6¾lb],
    boned
sea salt and freshly ground
    black pepper
10 tarragon sprigs
10 mint sprigs
bunch of flat-leaf parsley
6 garlic cloves, halved

Preheat the oven to 200°C/400°F/Gas 6.

Trim the lamb, cutting off any membrane and excess fat. Open up the meat so that it lies flat and sprinkle with salt and pepper. Place the herbs and garlic cloves in the middle, close the meat around the herbs and tie at intervals with kitchen string. Now rub the outside with some salt and pepper.

Place the lamb in a large roasting pan and roast for 1 hour 15–1 hour 30 minutes. Check the internal temperature using a thermometer: it should read 62°C/143°F for pink and 70°C/158°F for well done.

Leave to rest for 15 minutes before carving and serving with Curried beetroot and pumpkin (page 169).

Seared Romaine salad, bacon and Parmesan

When the fresh Romaine lettuce comes to Copenhagen in May, the heads
are perfect to serve fried or grilled. This makes a great lunch or starter.
If you are vegetarian, leave the bacon out and add some toasted walnuts instead.

Serves 4

100g [3½oz] rashers [slices]
   of bacon
3 small heads of Romaine or
   cos lettuce
1 Tbsp olive oil
sea salt and freshly ground
   black pepper
50g [2oz] Parmesan cheese,
   shaved into fine strips with
   a vegetable peeler
4 Tbsp cress
1 lemon, cut into wedges

Fry the bacon in a dry pan until crisp, then break it up
into smaller pieces.

Trim each head of lettuce, cut into quarters
lengthways, brush with the olive oil and sprinkle with
salt and pepper. Heat a griddle or a frying pan over
a high heat. Griddle or fry each segment of lettuce on
all sides, then place in serving dishes or bowls.

Evenly divide the bacon and Parmesan on top,
decorate with the cress and sprinkle with pepper.
Serve with lemon wedges.

Rundetårn

This tower is in the centre of the city. It was built by King Christian IV in the 17th century, and he was much involved in its construction. Uniquely in Europe, it has no stairs at all; instead it has a spiral walkway. As you can imagine, there are a lot of stories and myths about why this might be; my favourite is that the king wanted Rundetårn to be without stairs because he was too lazy to walk and wanted a horse-drawn carriage to take him all the way up to the observatory at the top! Though this is an enticing tale, there is no record of how this extraordinary building actually came about. There is a wonderful story that Russian Tsar Peter the Great rode the 281 metres up the tower's walkway on horseback, while the Tsarina took a carriage. It is a long and winding walk all the way up there to the observatory, but a beautiful one in this staircase-without-stairs, not least due to the blindingly whitewashed walls. In my opinion, it is one of Copenhagen's best attractions and really worth the stroll.

The narrow streets in the vicinity of the Rundetårn are lovely to walk around. You sense the presence of history through the old buildings: the student quarters, the **University** and churches such as **Vor Frue Kirke**. And it's easy to fuel your forays around the neighbourhood, as it is teeming with cafés and coffee bars. In the public library in Krystalgade is **Café Democratic**, which has some of the best croissants in town.

Next to the Rundetårn itself is a small square, one of my favourite spots for a hotdog as there's an organic **hotdog stand**. These small street-food trolleys are a common sight in Copenhagen; the first opened in January 1921 after a long, hard battle for official permission. Since then, hotdog stands have been a permanent part of the street scene in Danish towns, often referred to as 'cold feet restaurants'. Hotdogs are serious business here – there is even an annual hotdog competition (part of Copenhagen Cooking) in August. I love an old-school hotdog now and then, and sometimes I even manage to convince my husband to cycle with me to the square and have a hotdog (architecture is on my side here, because he loves the square).

So, what's the story with the Danish hotdog? Your first dilemma is how to order the sausage – steamed or pan-fried – and plain or red (these days, thankfully, dyed by healthy colourants). Now to the complicated bit: the multitude of condiments. Which of the two kinds of mustard – sweet or strong – should you choose, or perhaps you should try both? Do you want ketchup, rémoulade (page 55) or raw or fried onions (or both) with that? Or all of them? Do you want to top it off with cucumber salad (page 126)? It's a minefield. But the biggest problem is that you will undoubtedly eat it so fast that you'll then have to decide whether to have another…

Danish hotdogs

You can find hotdogs all over Copenhagen, in a lot of different varieties; this is the street food of the city. There is even a stall in the arrivals section at the airport, to greet homesick Copenhageners. A hotdog comes with a lot of condiments and everyone has their favourite combination. I like mine with ketchup, sweet mustard, cucumber and fried onions.

Makes 10

For the rolls
25g [1oz] fresh yeast
300ml [1¼ cups] lukewarm whole milk
50g [3½ Tbsp] salted butter
500g [3½ cups] strong white flour, plus more to dust
1 Tbsp sugar (any type)
1 tsp fine sea salt
1 egg, lightly beaten

For the cucumber salad
250ml [1 cup] apple cider vinegar
3½ Tbsp water
125g [⅔ cup] caster [granulated] sugar
pinch of sea salt
2 cucumbers

For the hotdogs
10 good-quality butcher's sausages
100g [3½oz] Fried onions (page 196)
4 Tbsp raw onions, chopped
tomato ketchup
sweet Scandinavian mustard
Rémoulade (page 55)

For the rolls, crumble the yeast into the milk and stir to dissolve. Melt the butter and stir it into the milk. Now mix in the flour, sugar and salt, then knead well on a floured surface. Put the dough into a bowl, cover with a tea towel and leave it to rise at room temperature for 1–2 hours, or until doubled in size. After it has risen, form into 10 fat oval buns and place on 2 baking sheets lined with baking parchment. Cover with tea towels and leave to rise for 20 minutes.

Now for the cucumber salad. Whisk the vinegar, water, sugar and salt together in a non-reactive bowl. Slice the cucumber thinly, add to the vinegar mixture and leave to stand for at least 30 minutes.

Preheat the oven to 180°C/350°F/Gas 4.

Brush the rolls with the egg and bake for 20–25 minutes. Leave to cool on a wire rack.

For the hotdogs, fry the sausages in a dry frying pan for 5–10 minutes, depending on their size, until cooked through. Meanwhile, get all the condiments ready. Now everyone just has to assemble their own hotdog to their liking!

The King's Garden

This is the oldest public garden in Copenhagen and I've been lucky enough to grow up here. I played here as a child, held hands while strolling the paths with my first boyfriend, enjoyed family picnics on the lawns, celebrated summer birthdays, taught my children to ride their bikes… and occasionally got so carried away that I was locked in after opening hours. Year after year I have enjoyed the rose garden, the great flowerbeds and the ever-changing seasons, all suffused with the wonderful light of Copenhagen.

The quirky small castle here, **Rosenborg**, was the summer residence 400 years ago of King Christian IV, and the gardens belonged to it, too. When you visit Rosenborg, it feels as though the royals just got up and left one day and never came back. That castle has been there in the background all my life. I went to school on the other side of the garden and we used the castle and its grounds for PE and play. Sometimes, when I was bored in class, I just gazed out of the window, looking into the King's Garden, following the seasons.

Hans Christian Andersen became a Copenhagener as a young man and lived in the centre of town. There is a statue of this gentle soul in the garden, where you can go to be reminded of his wonderful fairy tales. Those stories mean the world to me and I have read them over and again, so I like to walk by him often and always give him a small nod of recognition. The King's Garden appears in his work. In *Little Ida's Flowers*, the student tells Ida that the flowers are tired because they went to a ball at Rosenborg Castle. 'Haven't you often visited the garden just outside the gates, where the King lives in the summertime? You remember the place where swans swim close when you offer them breadcrumbs. Out there, that's where the real dancing is, believe me.' I took both my youngest sister and my daughter to the castle, read *Little Ida's Flowers* for them and then we walked around the castle and imagined Ida's flowers dancing there.

I always get off my bike on my way home to walk through the garden. Nothing is better than a stroll through the King's Garden at twilight, looking at the old castle while the setting sun casts its last rays before it disappears and the birds sing the day goodbye. It is truly magical and one of the many aspects of the city that make Copenhagen special for me.

Copenhageners love to be outdoors as soon as the weather permits, so at the slightest hint of spring it's like a cocoon opens up and there is activity everywhere. The King's Garden becomes full of people, on picnics, birthday parties and work outings, people with tablecloths and homemade food, or groups of girlfriends who have bought sushi and a bottle of wine from a shop. Before you enter from Gothersgade, have coffee and ice cream in **Kafferiet** near the garden walls.

Opposite, top: Rosenborg Castle
Opposite, bottom: Hans Christian Andersen

The seasons

Any traveller to Copenhagen will soon realize that in Denmark we have more than four seasons for the weather, produce, and just the feel of the days – maybe as many as eight or even ten. I love the winter, with its dark days and cold, especially when it snows because everything goes quiet and, all of a sudden, you sense the world around you in its entirety; not a sound interrupts you living in the moment. Spring is playful, teasing us about when it will arrive… just as the first tiny signs of new life show and we feel the slightest excitement, spring draws back and lets us wait. When it finally arrives the light is crisp, the colours almost blinding, the food bright and new. Then comes summer with warm sun, silent rain and thunderstorms, sweet berries and beach life and – in Scandinavia – long bright nights that feel as though they will never end. Autumn light is golden and provides the last warmth of the year before the dark falls once again, preparing you each day for the coming winter by gradually changing its colours and losing its leaves. Food is plentiful, earthy and comforting.

Right: Rosenborg Castle
Opposite: Statue of Hans Christian Andersen

Rye-crust tart with feta and leeks

Go to Torvehallerne and buy a tart and bread from Hahnemanns Køkken, charcuterie from Steensgaards ham and salami and cheese from Unika, then stroll over to the Royal Gardens and enjoy a great picnic.

Serves 4–6

For the pastry

100g [¾ cup] plain [all-purpose] flour, plus more to dust

100g [⅞ cup] wholegrain stoneground rye flour

1 tsp sea salt

75g [⅓ cup] chilled salted butter, plus more for the tin or dish

75g [⅓ cup] curd cheese or cream cheese

For the filling

4 leeks (about 600g/1lb 5oz)

3 garlic cloves, finely chopped

2 Tbsp olive oil

sea salt and freshly ground black pepper

6 medium eggs

200g [7oz] feta cheese, crumbled or chopped

200g [scant cup] cream cheese

¼ tsp ground cloves

Begin with the pastry. Mix both flours with the salt in a large bowl. Cut the butter into small cubes and rub it into the flour with your fingertips, then mix in the curd cheese or cream cheese. Knead the dough lightly with your hands just until the ingredients are combined. (Alternatively, pulse all the ingredients together in a food processor, adding a little water if the dough does not come together.)

Roll out the dough on a floured surface and butter a 28cm [11in] diameter tart tin or pie dish. Use the pastry to line the tin, then refrigerate for 1 hour, or overnight.

Preheat the oven to 180°C/350°F/Gas 4. Line the pastry case with baking parchment and pour in ceramic baking beans, dried beans or uncooked rice. Bake it for 15 minutes, then remove the beans (or rice) and parchment and bake for a further 5 minutes. Remove from the oven and increase the oven temperature to 200°C/400°F/Gas 6.

Meanwhile, for the filling, slice the leeks and rinse carefully. Drain well and sauté them and the garlic in the olive oil for 5 minutes. Pour out any excess moisture that has come from the leeks. Season with a little salt – remembering that the feta can be rather salty – and with pepper.

Beat the eggs together in a mixing bowl, then stir in the feta, cream cheese and cloves. Season the mixture, fold in the leeks and pour the mixture into the pastry case. Bake for 30–35 minutes, or until the filling has set but retains a slight wobble.

Serve with charcuterie.

Shops

I was lucky, as a child, to be able to step out of the hallway of our apartment and suddenly be in the midst of a busy town, a wonderful place to live. All the great shops were just around the corner, and the **King's Garden** (page 129) was a stone's throw away, yet at night it was surprisingly calm. Some of the shops from that time have closed and new ones have opened, but the two most important ones – from a food lover's point of view – are still there.

First, there is **Perch's tea room**, where I still buy my tea (and honey bombs when I don't bake them myself, see page 14). This family-run tea shop, with its very impressive selection, has been here since 1835 and you can still go upstairs next door to their tea room and take afternoon tea. I drink Perch's English breakfast tea every morning and in the evenings their Karen Blixen tea, which is a nice Earl Grey.

The second big attraction is the organic butcher on **Kultorvet**, locally known as 'the butcher with the bowler hats'. It is the first organic butcher in Copenhagen and I have been buying meat there for at least 25 years. They are true professionals, always maintaining a welcoming atmosphere combined with real craftsmanship. If you are not going to cook, go there and buy their homemade salami, a traditional Danish *spegepølse*, which is smoked rather than cured; it will keep for a long time. They also sell cold cuts and salads to go at lunchtime for the traditional *smørrebrød*. Their liver pâté, especially, is very good; try it on rye bread and topped with pickles for the classic Danish lunch called *madder*. (Or make your own – see page 115 for my recipe.)

Just around the corner from the butcher, you'll find an organic cheese shop with typical Danish cheeses. Don't miss the semi-hard cow's cheese **Danbo**, a breakfast classic – my favourite is the variety flavoured with cumin seeds – or **Vesterhavs** cheese with its touch of acidity, or smoked fresh cheese, or Danish brie from Knuthenlund.

Sømods Bolsjer is an iconic family-owned sweet shop that makes their own boiled sweets (*bolsjer*) in a small factory right in the middle of Copenhagen. You can also visit the factory to see how they do it. I think it is a fascinating craft: the process in which the sugar is melted, stretched and candy-striped is mesmerizing to see. My favourite flavours are rhubarb and green pear. The shop also sells big black liquorice-flavoured sweets known as *dameskrå*, – the name comes from the time when men would throw (*skrå*), which was not considered proper for ladies, so ladies had their own hard candy instead.

Restaurants

Instead of farm-to-table, restaurant **Wilhelm** works with a concept that goes from forest to table. For classic open sandwiches, **Gitte Kik** is legendary. **Ruby** is a bar whereby you are invited into a traditional Copenhagen flat to sip cocktails and feel at home. I love going there early before the crowds take over; you'll find some authentic *hygge*. For something lavish, go to **Trio** at the top of the new Axel Towers and experience the views over Copenhagen.

Left: Sømods Bolsjer

Spires of Copenhagen

All cities have their trademarks, and Copenhagen's iconic view (apart from the bikes) is the spires that give the skyline its characteristic profile. This is especially evident if you get a chance to view the city a little from above. There are spires on many of the churches, on the **Town Hall**, and on **Christiansborg Palace** (the parliament building). The spires are mostly covered with verdigrised copper, though on Christiansborg Palace, the copper has been replaced recently and is therefore still brown.

The building next to Christiansborg Palace is **Børsen**, the old chamber of commerce and stock exchange with its copper-covered spire. It used to be a small island surrounded by the sea, and way back in time, the canals were alive with trade and commodities were delivered to the stock exchange and traded there.

Close to both is the **Royal Library** and I recommend a visit to the garden there, where I spent many lunch breaks with my rye sandwiches and tea while studying literature at **Copenhagen University**. You share the garden with a statue of the philosopher **Søren Kierkegaard**, who looks thoughtful and reminds you that life must be lived forwards but can only be understood backwards.

Christiansborg Palace is huge, looming, dark and not very inviting. It is the parliament and centre of power, and the government resides in the surrounding buildings. It was built after the catastrophic fire of 1884 that destroyed the Christiansborg Palace (which itself was the second palace, due to an 18th-century fire).

In the great hall hangs a tapestry series by Danish artist Jørgen Nørgaard. It is quite impressive and tells the story of Danish history. There are guided tours twice a day; in the afternoon the tour is in English.

My company ran the restaurants in the Christiansborg for seven years and I really like the building from the inside! It has fabulous rooms, great halls and a true sense of history. We cooked some terribly good food for politicians, royals and international guests, but what I am most proud of is that I got into a great dialogue with the people who work there. We set them on a path to eat more vegetables, we had lunches where they brought their spouses and we talked about small changes to diet that we can all make without compromising on flavour.

Behind the palace is another favourite spot of mine: the royal riding grounds (see pages 138–139) – where they still train the queen's horses – and what is left of the **rococo palace**. It a shame that it burnt down. Copenhagen would have been more beautiful with the old Christiansborg. If you keep walking, you come to the canals. At night there is a tranquil atmosphere here, very calm; the light is dim, and it is easy to imagine the Copenhagen of hundreds of years ago.

Cross the canal and you'll find a very old part of the city. If only the cobbled streets could talk… There was a lively market in this area 200 years ago, and along the canal *fiskerkoner* ('fishwives') would sell their wares. They would wear special embroidered scarves and shawls. The last one stopped selling fish there in 2008.

Opposite: Copenhagen Town Hall
Pages 138–139: Christiansborg

Fishcakes with potatoes and Brussels sprouts

Fishcakes can be made in many different ways and can be found on most menus at traditional Danish lunch restaurants in Copenhagen. This recipe is quite classic, but spices and other herbs can also be added.

Serves 4–6

Cucumber salad (page 126)

For the rémoulade

1 carrot, finely chopped
120g [4½oz] celeriac [celery root], peeled and finely chopped
sea salt and ground black pepper
½ cucumber, deseeded and finely chopped
50ml [3½ Tbsp] good mayonnaise (see page 56 for homemade)
2 tsp medium curry powder
1 tsp ground turmeric
½ tsp mustard powder
2 tsp lemon juice
2 Tbsp capers, chopped

For the small baked potatoes

800g [1¾lb] small potatoes
2 Tbsp olive oil

For the fishcakes

600g [1lb 5oz] skinned cod fillet
1 onion, grated
3 medium eggs, lightly beaten
100ml [⅓ cup] whole milk
½ tsp freshly grated nutmeg
4 Tbsp chopped dill
1 Tbsp chopped tarragon leaves
2 Tbsp capers, chopped
5 Tbsp plain [all-purpose] flour
2–3 Tbsp salted butter

For the Brussels sprouts

400g [14oz] Brussels sprouts
1 Tbsp salted butter

Start with the rémoulade. Cook the carrot and celeriac in lightly salted boiling water for 2 minutes. Drain well and leave to cool. Mix them with the cucumber in a bowl. Mix all the other ingredients in another bowl, then fold into the carrot and celeriac mixture, seasoning to taste with salt and pepper.

Preheat the oven to 180°C/350°F/Gas 4.

For the baked potatoes, wash the potatoes, then mix them with the olive oil, salt and pepper. Put in a roasting pan and bake in the oven for 45 minutes.

Meanwhile, make the fishcakes. Finely chop the cod and use a very sharp knife or a food processor to mince it. Place it in a bowl with the onion, eggs, milk, nutmeg, dill, tarragon and capers. Fold all the ingredients together gently, then add the flour and 1 tsp each of salt and pepper and fold again.

Melt the butter in a big frying pan. Form the fishcake mixture into oval balls with a spoon and a hand. Place them gently in the butter over a medium heat and fry them for 7–8 minutes on each side. Now put them in a roasting pan and finish in the oven for 10 minutes.

Rinse the Brussels sprouts, then cut the bottom off each. Remove and reserve the outer leaves, then cut each sprout into quarters. Sauté the quarters in the butter for 3–4 minutes, then add the reserved leaves and sauté for 1 minute more, seasoning to taste with salt and pepper.

Serve the fishcakes with the potatoes, Brussels sprouts, rémoulade and cucumber salad.

Christmas

Christmas is a great time to visit Copenhagen, mainly because we *love* Christmas. You will find decorations everywhere. Of course, you get the stress and the bustle that is peculiar to the festive season here, just like you do anywhere else, but I believe the atmosphere is special, somehow heightened by our dark afternoons, candles twinkling in every corner and a sense of expectation hanging in the air. Christmas in Copenhagen is, for a lot of people, the quintessential *hygge* moment.

I have a lot of food and drink-related rituals that I reserve for December in the city. I like to drink *gløgg* and eat *æbleskiver* (page 148), bake saffron buns for Sankta Lucia Day and search for honey hearts in bakeries and chocolate shops, trying them all out and deciding which I like best, or discovering new ones. I go to Christmas lunches with friends, and drink the special Christmas beer brew that you'll find at all the cafés. So, if you visit Copenhagen in December, make sure you do all this… and don't forget to buy pepper cakes and other Christmas cookies, too!

I like a bit of decadence at Christmas: at this time of year I'm attracted to the lavish, the over-the-top. I allow myself to lose control a little, let the glitter come out, eat sweet chocolate, drink champagne (have a bit too much to eat and drink, in all honesty) and let the conversation continue into the early hours.

If you want to buy Christmas presents, **Illums Bolighus** is great for Scandinavian design and some of the best ceramics and china in Denmark. **Strædet**, the pedestrian street that runs parallel to **Strøget**, is also interesting and fun for shopping. There is an independent antiques store selling exclusively used **Royal Copenhagen** (see page 151). I can spend hours in there, looking and imagining all the dinner parties this china has seen. In this street, you'll also find a shop with **Danish Unika** ceramics.

Then, in December, we Danes spend an awful lot of time waiting for the snow. Unlike the British, we do not talk a lot about the weather… except in December. Nothing makes us happier than a white Christmas. Personally speaking, I wake up every day and throw open the curtains to look out the window. I obsessively read the weather forecast. If snow does fall in December, I get properly dressed, go into town immediately, stroll through the old streets and soak up the atmosphere, experiencing how the city just turns white and the silence slowly takes over.

Beer

Copenhagen has always been a beer town. Carlsberg's very first brewery was located in the centre before it moved out of town to Valby. It used to be that a Copenhagener had a preferred brand of beer that they would always drink, and into which they put a part of their identity. There were many breweries in the city. They merged over the course of 200 years into just two: Carlsberg and Tuborg, and in the end, only Carlsberg remained. Now, microbreweries are back, and cafés and restaurants are once again carrying interesting, different and smaller-batch beers. In December, everywhere sells a special Christmas beer, spiced or infused with the aromatics of the season, or even with fruit or liquorice and other more outlandish experiments.

Right, top left: Gråbrødretorv
Right, bottom right: Hotel d'Angleterre

Pork rillettes with apple topping

Stroll around the city and make sure to go through Gråbrødre Square and enjoy the tree in the middle. Eat a Christmas lunch at Aamanns, making sure to start with the excellent herrings and to taste some of their excellent *brændevin* (homemade aquavit).

Makes about 500g [1lb 2oz]

For the rillettes

250g [9oz] skinned, boned pork belly
250g [9oz] boned pork neck
2 cloves
1 onion, peeled
2 bay leaves
4 thyme sprigs
5 juniper berries, crushed (optional)
sea salt and freshly ground black pepper
rye bread (see page 264 for homemade), to serve

For the apple topping

1 tsp salted butter
1 red onion, finely sliced
2 eating apples, such as Cox
4 thyme sprigs
1 Tbsp capers
1 tsp sugar (any type)
1 Tbsp apple cider vinegar

For the rillettes, cut the meat into 3 x 1 x 1cm [$1\frac{1}{4}$ x $\frac{3}{8}$ x $\frac{3}{8}$in] strips and place them in a large, heavy-based saucepan. Slowly heat, stirring, until the fat begins to melt. Stick the cloves into the onion.

Add the remaining ingredients (except the rye bread) to the pork and cover with a lid. Let the meat simmer in its own fat over a very low heat for about 5 hours until very, very tender.

Remove the meat from the saucepan with a slotted spoon, discarding the bay leaves, thyme sprigs and onion. Tear it into very fine shreds using 2 forks, then season to taste with salt and pepper.

Pour the cooking liquid through a sieve [strainer] into a bowl and refrigerate until the fat has set.

Pack the meat tightly into sterilized jars (page 56) or a terrine mould. When the fat in the bowl has set, scrape it off, place it in a saucepan and heat until liquid. Pour the fat over the meat in the jars or terrine mould until the meat is completely covered with fat, to seal it from the air and preserve the rillettes. Leave overnight in the refrigerator, though it will now keep for several weeks.

Before serving the rillettes, make the apple topping. Melt the butter in a frying pan, add the sliced onion, then peel and core the apples and cut them, too, into thin slices and add right away to the pan so that they don't discolour. Add the thyme and capers and sauté for a few minutes, then sprinkle with the sugar, salt and pepper. Fold together gently, then add the vinegar and leave to simmer for 2 minutes. Leave to cool for a few minutes.

Serve the rillettes with the apple topping and rye bread.

Saffron buns

These buns are eaten in December, specifically on 13 December, Sankta Lucia Day. Nowadays, some bakeries make them all year round. I am too old-school for that, so I restrict my baking of them to December.

Makes 24

100ml [⅓ cup] boiling water
½ tsp saffron threads
50g [2oz] fresh yeast
400ml [1⅔ cups] lukewarm
    whole milk
200g [7oz] crème fraîche
200g [¾ cup plus 2 Tbsp] unsalted
    butter, melted and left to cool
    a little
1.1kg [8¼ cups] '00' flour
200g [1½ cups] raisins (optional)
5g [1 tsp] fine sea salt
200g [1 cup] caster [granulated]
    sugar
1 egg, lightly beaten

Mix the boiling water with the saffron, stir a little and leave for 10 minutes.

Crumble the yeast into the milk and stir to dissolve, then add the crème fraîche, melted butter and saffron water. In a separate bowl, mix 1kg [7½ cups] of the flour with the raisins (if using), salt and sugar, then mix into the yeast mixture. Knead with the rest of the flour on a surface into a smooth dough. Return to the bowl, cover and leave to rise in a warm place for 2 hours.

Form the buns by rolling the dough into 24 sausages, then curl each into a round bun. Alternatively, you could shape each as the numbers eight or five, or other shapes inspired by Nordic mythology.

Set on baking sheets lined with baking parchment, cover with tea towels and leave to rise again, in a warm place, for 30 minutes.

Preheat the oven to 200°C/400°F/gas mark 6. Brush the buns with the egg and bake for 25 minutes. Leave to cool on a wire rack before serving.

Æbleskiver with jam

You will find these served with *gløgg*, the warm mulled wine on offer all over town in December, and they definitely belong to the Christmas season. There are a lot of industrial versions and the real thing is hard to come by. I have to make them in December, otherwise it doesn't feel like Christmas.

Serves 8

40g [1½oz] fresh yeast
800ml [3⅓ cups] lukewarm
  whole milk
600g [4½ cups] plain [all-
  purpose] flour
2½ tsp fine sea salt
1½ tsp ground cardamom
2 vanilla pods [beans]
3 Tbsp caster [granulated] sugar
4 medium eggs, separated
150g [⅔ cup] butter
200g [7oz] prunes, pitted
  (optional)
icing [confectioner's] sugar,
  to dust
strawberry or raspberry jam,
  to serve

Crumble the yeast into the milk in a large bowl and stir to dissolve.

In another large bowl, sift together the flour, salt and cardamom. Slit the vanilla pods lengthways, scrape out the seeds with the tip of a sharp knife and add to the dry ingredients with the sugar.

Whisk the eggs yolks into the milk mixture. Add the dry ingredients and beat to make a dough.

In a separate bowl, whisk the egg whites until stiff, then fold them into the dough. Cover the bowl with a tea towel and leave to rest at room temperature for 40 minutes.

Heat an *æbleskiver* pan over a medium heat. Put a little butter in each indentation, and when it has melted, pour in some of the batter. Place half a prune (if using) in each and cook for 3–5 minutes, or until golden underneath, then turn the doughnuts over. Continue frying for about 4–5 minutes, or until golden, then remove. Repeat with the remaining batter. Dust with icing sugar and serve immediately with jam.

Royal Copenhagen's Christmas table

Royal Copenhagen's flagship store is in one of the oldest buildings in Copenhagen, on the pedestrian street **Strøget**. I am a loyal fan of Royal Copenhagen and I collect it, not to be hidden away in cupboards to gather dust, but to be used every day, to give me joy in my daily life. I highly recommend that you go and see the shop. When I clap my eyes on all the different plates, serving dishes, terrines and cups there, I just want to run home, cook a lavish dinner, set the table and invite lots of people. China makes food look amazing and a beautifully set table is the perfect backdrop to any great meal.

Royal Copenhagen was founded in 1755. For the first 100 years it was owned by the Danish royal family, before becoming a private company. Among the resolutions of the first board meeting on 1 May 1775 was that the factory's trademark should be three wavy lines, representing the three waterways that pass through Denmark: the Little Belt, the Great Belt and Øresund. The same trademark still adorns Royal Copenhagen's china. One day, my mother-in-law telephoned to announce that she wanted me to have her Royal Copenhagen china. Of course, I was thrilled. She told me, "It is because you set the table every day, with a home-cooked dinner, so I'd like you to use it every day."

Soon after its foundation, china by Royal Copenhagen was famous all over Europe. In 1801, the English bombarded Copenhagen, mainly because we sided with Napoleon and the English did not want Napoleon to get his hands on our fleet. After Lord Nelson had attacked Copenhagen, and just before he left for England with the Danish fleet, he sent his lieutenant into the city to pay a visit to Royal Copenhagen, to order a set of china for Lady Hamilton.

In Royal Copenhagen's flagship store each Christmas, there is an exhibition organized around the theme of the Christmas table. A group of people get a table each to present. It can be artists, writers, artisans or chefs. In 2017, the assignment was given to the Royal Danish Ballet. My favourite table that year was by the solo dancer Ida Prætorius, whose display was entitled: The After Party. It represented how she liked to wind down after the hard work and long hours and referred to places she visits with colleagues in both Copenhagen and New York. I immediately wanted to sit down at her table, to join in with Ida's colleagues and reflect on the day that had passed.

Opposite: 2017 Royal Christmas table at Royal Copenhagen's flagship store

Gammel Mønt

Some restaurants are not new and therefore not part of the buzz of all the new places in Copenhagen. It is interesting that most of the newest places are not in the centre but in the surrounding boroughs; that is starting to change and new places are starting to open up in the centre. Some eateries have been around for a long time and are still, after many years, great places to eat and drink.

At the intersection of the streets **Gammel Mønt** and **Møntergade**, you will find **Restaurationen** and **R Wine Bar**. The restaurant was here long before the 'new Nordic' hype (page 97) and before Copenhagen became a destination for gourmet travellers. Lisbeth and Bo Jacobsen cook modern Danish food – some would say with a French twist – served on Royal Copenhagen china. Originally it was fine dining; now it is brasserie style. For decades they have flown the flag for Danish tradition, working with quality produce and celebrating the importance of cooking as a craft. Lisbeth also makes great cakes and puddings.

The R Wine Bar has a great list, but you will probably not find cutting-edge natural wine; it is a bit more traditional. I love the old-school service, the cheese board and the charcuterie. Whenever my husband suggests going out for a drink and an adventure, we end up going to R and having a bite to eat and a few glasses of fantastic wine. Sometimes it's just nice to do something you already know… I find that relaxing in a very busy life.

Right: Restaurationen
Opposite: R Wine Bar

Spring veal fricassee

Here is your spring classic. Look out for asparagus in Copenhagen in May and June, whether the purple, green or white variety – all are delicious.

Serves 4

700g [1½lb] boned stewing veal, ideally from the shoulder
300g [10½oz] white asparagus spears
300g [10½oz] green asparagus spears
30g [2 Tbsp] salted butter
300ml [1¼ cups] white wine
500ml [2 cups] water
2 carrots, cut into large chunks
2 celery stick, cut into 3 pieces
2 bay leaves
5 thyme sprigs
10 white peppercorns
2 tsp sea salt
handful of chervil sprigs, to serve
1kg [2¼lb] new potatoes, boiled, to serve

For the velouté
35g [2½ Tbsp] salted butter
35g [¼ cup] plain [all-purpose] flour
120ml [½ cup] double [heavy] cream
sea salt and freshly ground white pepper
3 spring onions [scallions], thinly sliced
300g [2 cups] podded peas

Cut the veal into 3cm [1¼in] cubes.

Peel the white asparagus spears, reserving the trimmings. Break off and discard the lowest part of both the white and green spears: if you bend them, they will naturally snap at the correct place. Keep the woody ends as well as the tender spears.

Heat the butter in a large saucepan, add the meat and cook, turning, until browned on all sides. Add the white wine and water and gradually bring to the boil, skimming off any froth from the surface. Add the carrots, celery, the woody ends of the asparagus and the white asparagus peelings, the bay leaves, thyme sprigs, peppercorns and salt. Return to the boil, then reduce the heat and leave to simmer for 1 hour, or the meat is until very tender.

Strain the contents of the saucepan through a sieve [strainer] into a large bowl. Discard the vegetables and herbs, but keep the meat warm. Bring 700ml [3 cups] of the stock to the boil in a small saucepan. (You can freeze any remaining stock for a sauce or stew.)

Meanwhile, make the velouté. Melt the butter in a heavy-based saucepan. Whisk in the flour and cook for 1–2 minutes until it is foaming and straw-coloured. Remove the pan from the heat and whisk in one-third of the boiling stock. Bring the sauce to the boil, whisking constantly until it thickens, then add the remaining stock. Let the sauce simmer for at least 15 minutes, stirring now and then. Add the cream and simmer for 2 minutes, then season to taste with salt and white pepper. Add the veal.

Slice each asparagus spear into 3 and add to the pan with the spring onions. Simmer for 3–4 minutes, adding the peas for the last minute. Season to taste with salt, sprinkle with the chervil and serve with new potatoes.

Veal birds (Benløse fugle)

Benløse fugle means 'birds without bones'. This odd name probably comes from the flavours, which are similar to those that were once used to stuff chickens, pigeons and so on in the old days. You will need cocktail sticks.

Serves 4

For the beef
800g [1¾lb] beef topside, cut into 8 slices
sea salt and freshly ground black pepper
handful of flat-leaf parsley leaves, chopped
4 Tbsp thyme leaves
100g [3½oz] celeriac [celery root]
100g [3½oz] carrots
100g [3½oz] lard, cut into 8 slices, each about 3 x 0.5cm [1¼ x ¼in]
plain [all-purpose] flour, to dust
3 Tbsp salted butter
300–400ml [1¼–1⅔ cups] veal stock or water
1 Tbsp redcurrant jelly
100ml [⅓ cup] double [heavy] cream
lingonberry jam, to serve

For the mash
800g [1¾lb] potatoes
bunch of flat-leaf parsley
bunch of chives
50g [3½ Tbsp] salted butter

For the beef, place the slices of meat between 2 sheets of clingfilm [plastic wrap] and press each to 1cm [⅜in] thick with your palm. Sprinkle with salt and pepper and the parsley and thyme.

Peel and cut the celeriac and carrots into strips the same length as the meat slices. First place a slice of lard on each slice of topside and then divide the celeriac and carrot strips evenly on the fat. Roll the meat around the filling and close the roll with a cocktail stick [toothpick]. Roll in flour until completely covered.

Melt the butter in a saucepan until golden and bubbling briskly, then brown the rolls well on all sides. Add the stock or water and slowly bring to the boil, then cover with a lid and simmer for 1 hour.

Remove the *benløse fugle* from the saucepan and keep them warm. Add the redcurrant jelly and cream to the stock, bring to the boil and cook until thickened, seasoning to taste with salt and pepper. Put the *benløse fugle* back in the gravy and keep warm over a very low heat.

Meanwhile, for the mash, peel the potatoes and cut them into large cubes. Place in a large saucepan, cover with water and bring to the boil, then simmer until tender. Chop the parsley leaves and chives. Drain the potatoes, reserving about 150ml [⅔ cup] of their cooking liquid. Mash the potatoes with a balloon whisk – the mixture should be a little lumpy – then add the butter and 100ml [⅓ cup] of the reserved potato cooking liquid. Stir with a spoon, adding the herbs and a little more cooking liquid if needed. Season to taste with salt and pepper.

Serve the *benløse fugle* with the mash and some lingonberry jam on the side.

La Glace

High streets and pedestrian streets are, in most cities, not very charming, just full of a lot of the same chain stores. This goes for Copenhagen, too, and for that reason I do not enjoy the pedestrian street that leads from the Town Hall square up to Helligånds Church. But in the middle, just a few feet off the beaten track, is an iconic destination that is really worth a visit. It is **La Glace**, Copenhagen's oldest *konditori*.

When you enter La Glace, it feels like time travelling. When I am there, I am also forcibly reminded that Copenhagen is a European city. *Konditories* have been meeting spots for society for the last 200 years, places people liked to see and be seen, where those of importance would meet to discuss world issues.

I am not sure La Glace serves that purpose any more, but it is still a place for tradition, birthdays and other celebrations, a venue that proudly holds up a standard for the craftsmanship of cake baking. It is also famous for its ice-cream cakes, which come in many shapes and sizes. The window displays change and have special themes during the year. At Christmas there is always a queue outside, just to peer in and see the display, made up of both tourists and Danish families alike.

When I go, I always order the hot chocolate and soft buns with butter, though there is a range of layer cakes. One of the most famous is the 'sports' layer cake, a fantastical confection of a macaroon base, lots of whipped cream and caramelized choux puffs (page 163).

Hot chocolate with sweet raisin buns

I do not think there is anything that can give you more pleasure on a cold day, especially after a long walk, than hot chocolate and buns. Make sure to use good-quality chocolate.

Makes about 18

For the buns
25g [1oz] fresh yeast
600ml [2½ cups] cold water
5g [1 tsp] fine sea salt
2 Tbsp honey
250g [2⅛ cups] white stoneground spelt flour, plus more to dust
250g [2⅛ cups] wholegrain stoneground spelt flour
150g [1 cup] raisins
1 egg, lightly beaten
salted butter, to serve

For the hot chocolate
1 litre [4¼ cups] whole milk
125g [4½oz] dark [bittersweet] chocolate, about 60% cocoa solids, finely chopped
caster [granulated] sugar, to taste
250ml [1 cup] double [heavy] cream, whipped, to serve

Start with the buns. Crumble the yeast into the water in a big bowl, stir to dissolve, then add the salt and honey. Mix in the flours and give a good stir with a wooden spoon. Knead the dough lightly in the bowl, working in the raisins as you do so. Cover with clingfilm [plastic wrap] and leave to rise at room temperature for 1 hour.

Knead the dough gently on a generously floured surface, then form it into 18 buns. Place them on baking sheets lined with baking parchment. Cover with tea towels and allow to rise in a warm place for 30 minutes.

Preheat the oven to 220°C/425°F/Gas 7.

Brush the rolls with the egg. Spray cold water in the oven to create steam, then bake the rolls for 20 minutes. Leave to cool on a wire rack.

While the buns are cooling, make the hot chocolate. Slowly heat the milk in a saucepan until almost boiling, add the chopped chocolate and stir until it has dissolved. Taste and add some sugar, if you like.

Serve the buns and salted butter with mugs of hot chocolate, topped with the whipped cream.

Copenhagen cakes

These are inspired by an iconic cake they make at La Glace called 'sports cake' (page 159). It has nothing to do with sports, but there has always been a tradition in Copenhagen of naming cakes after famous people and events. This one was named after a late-19th-century political play called *Sports Men*. Here, I have focused on the choux pastry and a very simple cream, so they are easy to make at home, but they don't take the place of the real thing.

Makes 8

For the choux pastry
100g [7 Tbsp] salted butter,
    plus more for the baking sheet
200ml [¾ cup plus 1 Tbsp] water
100g [¾ cup] plain [all-purpose]
    flour
1 tsp caster [granulated] sugar
pinch of fine sea salt
3 medium eggs, lightly beaten

For the filling
150g [¾ cup] caster [granulated]
    sugar
300ml [1¼ cups] double [heavy]
    cream
2 Tbsp icing [confectioner's] sugar,
    plus more to dust

Start by making the choux pastry. Put the butter in a saucepan with the water and let it melt over a gentle heat. Now increase the heat and bring to the boil. Meanwhile, sift the flour, sugar and salt into a bowl. Take the pan off the heat, add the flour mixture and stir with a wooden spoon until a smooth paste is formed. Beat until it comes away from the sides of the pan and forms a ball, then remove from the heat and cool for 10 minutes.

Preheat the oven to 200°C/400°F/Gas 6.

Add the eggs to the dough a little at a time, beating well after each addition, until the mixture is smooth and glossy. You may not need all the egg. Put the dough in a piping [pastry] bag fitted with a 1cm [⅜in] star nozzle [tip]. Pipe several 5cm [2in] lines of choux pastry on to a baking sheet lined with buttered baking parchment until you run out of dough. Make sure you leave some space between the lines of dough.

Bake for 20–30 minutes; do not open the oven door for the first 10 minutes, or the pastry may not rise. The pastries are done when they are golden brown and firm. Transfer to a wire rack and, with a sharp knife, pierce holes in the side of each, to let the steam out. Leave to cool.

For the filling, heat the sugar in a heavy-based saucepan until it is melted and golden brown, then pour out on to a piece of baking parchment. Allow to cool and set, then break up into small pieces. Whip the cream until light and fluffy, then mix it with the icing sugar and caramel pieces.

Cut each choux pastry in half lengthways and pipe the cream over the bottom halves. Lightly press the tops over the cream, dust with icing sugar and serve.

Blackcurrant roulade

---

*I really like this freshly made and with homemade jam in winter,
or in the summer with fresh berries.*

Serves 6–8

unsalted butter, for the tin

For the roulade
3 medium eggs
125g [⅔ cup] caster [granulated]
 sugar, plus 2 Tbsp
125g [1 cup] plain [all-purpose]
 flour
2 tsp baking powder
50ml [3½ Tbsp] whole milk

For the cream
400g [14oz] blackcurrant jam
3 gelatine leaves
250ml [1 cup] double [heavy]
 cream

Preheat the oven to 180°C/350°F/Gas 4. Line a 40 x 30cm [16 x 12in] Swiss roll tin [jelly roll pan] with baking parchment and butter it lightly.

For the roulade, whisk the eggs and the 125g [⅔ cup] sugar with an electric whisk until pale and increased in volume to a pale mousse. Sift in the flour and baking powder; don't skip this step, as it's very important to sift the flour to get the correct, airy result. Gently fold the flour mixture into the egg mixture, then gently fold in the milk. Pour the batter into the prepared tin and spread it out evenly. Bake for 10 minutes, or until it springs back to the touch of a finger. Remove from the oven, sprinkle with the 2 Tbsp sugar and leave to cool on a wire rack .

For the cream, blitz the jam a bit in a food processor so that it becomes more like a paste. Place in a small saucepan and set over a gentle heat until it melts.

Meanwhile, soak the gelatine leaves in cold water for about 10 minutes to soften up, then lift them out of the water and stir into the hot blackcurrant jam, stirring well to dissolve evenly. Let the mixture cool to room temperature. Whip the cream until it billows, then fold it into the blackcurrant jam.

Turn the cake over, peel off and discard the baking parchment and spread the cream evenly over it, leaving 1cm [⅜in] of the edges uncovered. Now roll it up from one long side into a roulade. Wrap the roll tightly in baking parchment and leave to chill in the refrigerator for at least 2 hours, then cut into slices and serve.

Torvehallerne

On the outskirts of Copenhagen centre – just outside the site of the old city wall – you will find Torvehallerne, Copenhagen's food halls. The location is fitting, as it was home to the city's greengrocer's market from the 1890s onwards. Later, it became a smaller neighbourhood fruit and veg market that predated the organic and local food movements; it simply sold vegetables in abundance from Denmark and more widely from Europe. One of my classmate's parents had a stall there, among the serried ranks of neatly arranged produce. The place always had a special atmosphere, simultaneously tempting and a touch alarming, with stallholders crying their lungs out as they shouted their daily specials. As the day went on, prices fell and there were usually real bargains to be had by closing time.

After a temporary closure for various reasons and a long debate with City Hall on whether Copenhagen needed extra parking spaces more than it needed a food market, we finally got our food halls; they opened in 2011. The stalls are a mixture of seasonal fresh produce from local farms, groceries, fresh fish and meat, fancy French cheeses and smoked and fresh fish and cheeses from Bornholm, the Danish island in the Baltic Sea, but there are also street-food joints, bakeries with great cakes, wine bars and beer halls. Friday afternoons at the food halls are always fun and lively, with lots of activities, often based around different seasonal themes.

My company, **Hahnemanns Køkken**, opened up a stall in Torvehallerne in late 2017.

We sell my cookbooks as well as salads, bread, cakes and local produce from some of our favourite organic farmers. It's like a modern corner shop, where you can buy a bit of everything, but in this modern incarnation the 'everything' is all homemade and organic. I have always wanted to be part of the food halls and am delighted to be there now, enjoying my latest food adventure.

In the following pages are a selection of recipes for salads that we serve in our stall in the food halls. We change the salads weekly, they are 100% organic and as many as the vegetables as possible come from local farms.

A day out in Torvehallerne

If you start early, grab a coffee at **Coffee Collective** or **ReTreat**, then move on to **Grød** for a really good portion of morning porridge. Nothing is better than this comforting, smooth, warm start to the day (see page 224 for porridge recipes). If the sun is out, you can sit outside while you eat.

If you are planning to visit for lunch, there are plenty of options: try a confit de canard sandwich, the famous tacos from **Hija de Sanchez** (see also page 194), pizza, *smørrebrød*, hotdogs, juices or salads.

I often bicycle to Torvehallerne to buy groceries for dinner, or to pick up local cheeses, organic eggs and cold cuts, herrings from Bornholm, liquorice, chocolate, beer or mustard.

Curried beetroot and pumpkin

Serves 4

400g [14oz] beetroot [beet]
300g [10½oz] Hokkaido pumpkin
2 Tbsp hot Madras curry powder
4–5 Tbsp olive oil
sea salt and freshly ground
   black pepper
2–3 Tbsp lime juice
chopped fresh parsley, to serve

Preheat the oven to 180°C/350°F/Gas 4.

Peel the beetroot. Halve the pumpkin, scrape out the seeds and wash the skin well, then cut both the beetroots and pumpkin into 2cm [¾in] chunks. Mix the curry powder, olive oil and salt and pepper with the vegetables and spread out in a roasting pan.

Bake for 30–40 minutes, or until the vegetables are soft but not overcooked. Pour over the lime juice, add the parsley and season to taste with salt and pepper.

Red cabbage, apple and walnuts

Serves 4

For the salad
400g [14oz] red cabbage
2 Cox apples
50g [2oz] walnuts

For the dressing
1 Tbsp Dijon mustard
1 Tbsp honey
3 Tbsp apple cider vinegar
2 Tbsp walnut oil
sea salt and freshly ground
   black pepper

For the salad, remove the core from the cabbage, then shred the leaves. Core the apples and cut into thin wedges.

Toast the walnuts in a dry frying pan for a few minutes, then chop.

Whisk all the dressing ingredients together in a bowl and season to taste with salt and pepper. Mix through the salad and serve.

Cavolo nero and Jerusalem artichokes

I started making full-meal salads in the mid-1990s and built a whole company around the idea in Copenhagen. Jerusalem artichokes and cavolo nero are great vegetables for them, and this is one of my classic recipes.

Serves 4

2 red onions
juice of 1 lemon
2 tsp caster [granulated] sugar
sea salt and freshly ground
    black pepper
300g [10½oz] Jerusalem
    artichokes
2 Tbsp olive oil, plus 1 Tbsp
2 Tbsp white wine vinegar
100g [½ cup] pearled rye grains
400g [14oz] cavolo nero, coarse
    stalks removed

Peel and halve the onions, then slice them 1cm [⅜in] thick. Place them in a bowl with the lemon juice, sugar, salt and pepper. Leave to stand for at least 30 minutes before using.

Preheat the oven to 180°C/350°F/Gas 4.

Wash the Jerusalem artichokes thoroughly, but keep the peel on, then cut each in half and mix with the 2 Tbsp of olive oil, salt and pepper. Place on a baking sheet and bake for 30 minutes, then drizzle with the vinegar and leave to cool.

Cook the rye in boiling water for about 25–30 minutes, or until soft, then drain and rinse in cold water.

Rinse the cavolo nero, drain well and chop roughly. Heat the remaining 1 Tbsp olive oil in a frying pan and sauté the cavolo nero until it softens.

Mix everything together in a big bowl and season to taste with salt and pepper.

Brussels sprouts, cavolo nero and grapes

At a dinner at my house with a group of my female employees, Mie, a then-apprentice, made this wonderful salad. I stole the recipe immediately and it is now part of my autumn repertoire.

Serves 4

500g [1lb 2oz] Brussels sprouts
200g [7oz] cavolo nero, coarse
    stalks removed
200g [7oz] black seedless grapes
50g [2oz] hazelnuts
3–4 Tbsp extra virgin olive oil
sea salt and freshly ground
    black pepper
2–3 Tbsp lemon juice

Rinse the Brussels sprouts and cavolo nero, then drain well. Halve the sprouts, then remove the outer leaves. Roughly chop the cavolo nero and halve the grapes.

Toast the hazelnuts in a dry frying pan for about 3–4 minutes, then leave to cool and chop roughly.

Sauté the sprouts and cavolo nero in the olive oil in a sauté pan for 5 minutes. Season with salt and pepper, then remove from the pan with a slotted spoon and place in a bowl.

In the same sauté pan, fry the grapes in the oil for 2 minutes, then add them to the bowl along with the hazelnuts. Season to taste with lemon juice.

Botanical Gardens

These gardens are part of the park belt around Copenhagen city centre and are located just behind the **King's Garden** (page 129). This ring of parks – a wonderful green 'lung' for the city – is one of the many things for which we Copenhageners have to thank architect Ferdinand Meldahl. When the city wall and fortifications were removed in the mid-19th century, and Copenhagen opened up to the land behind its wall, Meldahl insisted on creating a green belt, saving parts of the fortifications and using some bits of its moat as lakes for the parks.

This means that we have **Øster Anlæg** in the east (page 246), the **Botanical Gardens** in the middle, then **Ørstedsparken** as the next one over towards the west. Together, they bring a fantastic openness to the centre of the city. They allow you to have a break from the traffic and noise, and provide places for people to hang out, relax and even feel a bit of closeness to nature. The parks create a sense of space and make the city very liveable.

The Botanical Gardens are a treasury of biodiversity and exotic plants. You can't take your bike with you through the gardens (even if you dismount), so you have to plan to walk. I am always amazed how many people are in there and how beautiful it is. It has alleys that lead to little secret places, where you can sit with your book or your lunch or, as I do, simply hide to enjoy a 30-minute pause, away from the world, pretending that time stands still within this seeming wilderness. The gardens are a breathing space that breaks up the fast pace of the city.

The Botanical Gardens are also university gardens with more than 10,000 plants, the botany student's raw material. It is, therefore, also the park with the most rules: no drinking, no bikes, dogs, jogging or topless sunbathing. Despite these rather strict regulations, as a young teenager I climbed the fence and walked around with my friends. I was really scared, though I didn't want to admit it, mostly because I was terrible at climbing fences and was nervous that I would never get back out again!

Here you can appreciate an impressive collection of plants, trees and landscapes from around the world. There is a stunning greenhouse, the **Palm House**, built in 1874. It is in a majestic setting, and has a lovely view from its staircase. As soon as you enter, you feel immediately lost and as though you've walked into a kind of Alice in Wonderland universe, with strange smells and unknown plants with names you've never heard of and have a hard time imagining how to pronounce.

In summer, there is a **coffee truck** where you can sit outside. In July and August there are guided tours around the gardens in English.

Opposite: The Palm House in the Botanical Gardens

Latin Quarter, Sankt Peders Stæde

In the 1980s, when I was young, this was the place to hang out. The people who had flats here were – in my mind – the coolest and luckiest folk on earth. It is interesting how your perspective changes…

Here were all the bars and clubs of the punk movement, second-hand shops, record stores, great street parties… a lot of life going on, 24 hours a day. It was the only place where you could buy a slice of pizza all through the night. The local baker opened around 6A.M., so you could also bring home bread for breakfast. We often knocked at the back door of the bakery, if they were not yet open, and bought freshly baked pastries directly from the baker himself to eat on our way home after a long night out.

Floss Bar was legendary at that time: a magnet for artists, punks and other riffraff! I spent many hours there with my friends and we always drank Guld Tuborg, the beer with the golden lady on the label. I haven't been there for years, but when I walk by it doesn't seem to have changed much since those days.

Nowadays you'll also find a really good coffee bar here: **Risteriet**. They make great coffee, but I also like to buy coffee beans there. When I was young, we did not have such a wide selection of coffee, and neither was it as good as it is now. Back then, we were just excited if a place didn't only serve filter coffee!

Left: Gold Tuborg artwork outside Floss Bar
Opposite: Teglgårdstræde

Vesterbro & Frederiksberg

As the name reveals, Vesterbro is the west borough, a former working-class neighbourhood containing the red light and meatpacking districts, the main railway station and cheap housing, but – on its broad boulevards and main streets – also boasting grand apartments. For many generations, this was the haunt of a mix of workers, students, drunks, drug addicts, prostitutes and immigrants, but it was the first area in Copenhagen to experience full-scale gentrification from the 1990s. Now, Vesterbro is buzzing with hipsters and fancy places have opened on every corner. As you might expect, the price of even a humble apartment here has skyrocketed in recent times.

I have lived here twice: the first time in the mid-1980s, in a classic two-bedroom flat with a lavatory fitted into the back staircase and a kitchen fit for only one person; then in a commune in one of the large eight-bedroom apartments, with a view over the railway station and central Copenhagen.

Before the neighbourhood changed, Vesterbro was a very busy area and it always had the best ethnic food. I especially remember a small local Thai restaurant, where I ate chicken in green curry for the first time. You almost walked into the kitchen on your way to the dining room, and you could spot the grandmother of the family standing on a green plastic box normally used for milk bottles, stirring big pots of curries for the evening guests. The diners were a mixture of folk: students like me, girls working the street with their dodgy boyfriends, taxi drivers and (of course) Copenhagen's Thai community. Just the aromas of this other world were enough for me to crave the food; luckily it wasn't pricey, so we ate here often.

Vesterbro's colourful history has its own literature: the famous Danish writers Tove Ditlevsen and Dan Turèll both lived here and wrote about it. Ditlevsen tells us about her childhood growing up in the backyards of this rough area, but also created novels and poems full of Vesterbro characters and interesting people. I first read her work with a young woman's existential pain and identified with the stories; she was a heroine for many of us in the 1970s.

Frederiksberg

Frederiksberg is a district on the border with Vesterbro. Nobody could miss that this is a different area, as the atmosphere changes significantly when you cross into this neighbourhood. The trees are old, the whole area just seems greener and the grand boulevard is inspired by Paris architecture. It leads up to the Frederiksberg Garden and palace. There are large villas, grand apartment blocks and a local independent shop environment that is inspiring. It is an area with a lot of patriotism, and there are some truly great spots.

Walk up along **Frederiksberg Allé** and try the ice cream from **Frederiksberg Chokolade**, and at the same time buy their *flødeboller* (page 234). It is made the classic way, which I prefer. Take a stroll through the streets with residential mansion houses. I really recommend treating yourself to dinner at the **Formel B** restaurant. Eat breakfast at **Sokkelund**. On Saturdays there is a great antiques fair in front of the town hall.

Opposite: Hotel Central & Café – the world's smallest hotel!

Værnedamsvej

This is a legendary street on the border between **Vesterbro** and posher **Frederiksberg** with its villas, grand apartments and beautiful **Frederiksberg Garden**. Værnedamsvej was probably the first food street ever in Copenhagen, with a great selection of bread, wine, fish and cheese on sale. Now other types of shop have opened as well, including fancy designer places.

I used to go to high school here in the 1980s. We would buy our lunch from the small shops, and I also loved to buy supplies of great-quality fish and cheese, though I could only do this at the start of the month when I had just got paid (a mixture of my government allowance and my part-time job), as I always ended up spending way too much money. I dreamed of being able to afford good food like this all the time.

One afternoon I was in the cheese shop. My classmate's father had just bought her a fancy new car, a Volkswagen Beetle with a leather soft top. She was so busy showing off, driving with the top down, waving to her friends, that she drove straight into a large parked beer truck. She smashed up the car, but was not hurt, so it was a farce rather than a tragedy. I often think about that event when I am back in this street shopping; how the city in which you grew up has scars and stories that you've experienced.

These days I mostly go to Værnedamsvej to buy Danish novels, because there is a great bookshop – **Thiemers Magasin** – on a side street. (They also stock English novels.) I go and get a coffee and sit in the window, chat with owner Rikke about the latest books and book news, and get lost in the world of books. Spending time in book stores and buying books is my biggest luxury in life. When I visit a new city, I can browse in the local book store for hours and time stops for me. Even in cities I know well, I like to visit familiar book stores. I love to be in cities where I do not speak the language, just so I can see which authors I know have been translated!

Round the corner from Værnedamsvej is **Central Hotel & Café** – the world's smallest hotel! It is just so charming; what a great use for this doll's house with its solitary room over a lovely coffee bar.

You'll find **Lidkøeb** bar in the unlikely location of the backyard of a small house in Vesterbro, on **Vesterbrogade**. My favourite time to go there is after an afternoon movie, in the early evening, just before it gets too busy.

Coffee

Coffee in Copenhagen is good, and there are a lot of independent coffee shops that take coffee very seriously. Filter coffee is the tradition here, and in the 1970s the café culture started in Copenhagen and coffee became more than just 'with milk'. I have been drinking coffee since I was about five years old. Nothing beats a really good cup of filter coffee. Look for Coffee Collective or Original Coffee.

Clockwise from top left: Thiemers Magasin; Central Hotel & Café; Thiemers Magasin; and Helges Ost cheese shop

Chicken in horseradish and fennel sauce

A winter dish, when cold weather makes you long for warming flavours. Traditionally, horseradish is one of the few spicy ingredients we use.

Serves 4

For the chicken
1 organic chicken
1 small onion, halved
1 carrot, halved
1 leek, cut into chunks
3 bay leaves
1 Tbsp black peppercorns
1 Tbsp coarse sea salt
1kg [2¼lb] new potatoes,
    boiled, to serve

For the sauce
20g [1½ Tbsp] salted butter
4 celery sticks, about 250g [9oz],
    finely sliced
1 fennel bulb, finely sliced
2 Tbsp plain [all-purpose] flour
200ml [¾ cup] double [heavy]
    cream
50g [2oz] freshly grated
    horseradish
4 Tbsp finely chopped chives
sea salt and freshly ground
    black pepper
flat-leaf parsley, to serve

Place the chicken in a large flameproof casserole dish and cover with cold water, then bring to the boil. Let it boil for 5 minutes. Remove any scum from the surface, then add the onion, carrot, leek, bay leaves, peppercorns and sea salt. Return to the boil, then reduce the heat and simmer for 1 hour. Lift the chicken from the broth and leave to cool. Strain the broth and save 800ml [3⅓ cups] for the sauce.

For the sauce, melt the butter in a large saucepan, add the celery and fennel and sauté for 2 minutes. Sprinkle the flour over the vegetables and stir to combine. Now add the chicken broth little by little, stirring all the time, until you have a smooth sauce. Add the cream and bring to the boil, then reduce the heat and simmer for 5 minutes.

Remove the skin and bones from the chicken and tear it into pieces. Add the chicken to the sauce and simmer until the meat is heated through. Remove from the heat, add the horseradish and chives and season to taste with salt and pepper. Serve with the boiled new potatoes and fresh parsley.

The meatpacking district

When I started my first catering company in 1996, I would visit the meatpacking district (**Kødbyen**) early every morning to pick up produce. I would arrive just before 6A.M. to be ready when the doors opened to the warehouse. I met the same characters every morning: there were the well-known *smørrebrød* people, who bought everything ready-made even though they always sold it as 'homemade' on their menu; and the big butcher guy with a very red face, who looked like his blood pressure needed checking. His wife was always with him, flashing more diamond rings than I could count and, in the winter, wearing a big mink coat that made her almost disappear. We would chat briefly about how busy we were – they were always complaining even though they did not seem to be missing out in life – before rushing in to snatch a cup of coffee and buy the goods we needed.

This was before anybody knew that the meatpacking district was going to be a fancy nightlife area, with great restaurants, bars and festivals – altogether an entirely different scene from the simple workplace it was for decades. There are still big statues left here, which tell the story of the neighbourhood: that all the meat in Copenhagen came through here before going out to shops and restaurants.

And, despite the area's transformation, there are still a handful of the old shops left: my fishmonger, a few butchers and a small place that turns out toppings for open sandwiches.

Today, you can visit some of Copenhagen's top galleries here, eat burgers, try Indian fast food or authentic tacos, eat late-night pizza or visit the street-food market on Saturdays. You can while away a whole day and stay late into the night, too.

Fiskebaren

You would think that, in a country with a long coastline, where nowhere is more than an hour's drive from the sea, you would eat a lot of fish. You would think that in that country's capital city, situated on the water with a harbour right in the city centre, you would find a large variety of fish restaurants. Sadly, this is not the case. We have only a few, and **Fiskebaren** is the one I know best. I like to sit in the bar and just eat mussels with a glass of wine, no fuss. When lumpfish roe is in season in early spring, I like to indulge in this Danish delicacy – our Nordic caviar, some say – served in the traditional style, either with onion and crème fraîche, or potatoes and smoked cheese.

Opposite: Kødbyens Fiskebar

Mussels with bacon, potatoes and tarragon

We call these 'blå muslinger', or blue mussels. We have a lot of them,
they are cheap and we ought to eat them weekly.

Serves 4

1kg [2¼lb] mussels
2 Tbsp olive oil
50g [2oz] bacon, finely chopped
1 onion, finely chopped
100g [3½oz] potatoes, skins on,
    scrubbed and finely chopped
3 garlic cloves, finely chopped
3–4 tarragon sprigs, plus a small
    handful of tarragon leaves
    to serve
300ml [1¼ cups] wheat beer
sea salt and freshly ground
    black pepper
crusty bread, to serve

Rinse the mussels in cold water. Scrub them thoroughly
and tug out any beards that may be hanging from the
shells. Discard any broken mussels, or those that are
open and refuse to close when tapped against the
edge of the sink. Keep them in the refrigerator until
you are ready to cook.

Heat the oil in a large saucepan, add the bacon and
cook until crisp, then add the onion, potatoes, garlic
and the tarragon sprigs. Now tip in the mussels,
pour in the beer and season with salt and pepper,
remembering that the mussels are salty.

Bring to the boil, then reduce the heat, cover and
steam for a few minutes, shaking the pan from time to
time, until all the mussels have opened. Discard the few
that refuse to open. Serve sprinkled with the tarragon
leaves and offer bread to soak up the delicious juices.

Monkfish in butter with spinach and rye

I recommend eating fish while you are in Copenhagen – there is a lot of lovely fresh fish here. Some of the best places to eat it are Kødbyens Fiskebar, Musling or Restaurationen. Then when you're back home, make this!

Serves 4

200g [1 cup] pearled rye grains
4 monkfish steaks, or a piece of tail
    big enough for 4 people
sea salt and freshly ground
    black pepper
2 Tbsp olive oil
1 red onion, finely sliced
1 garlic clove, finely chopped
½ tsp freshly grated nutmeg
2 Tbsp salted butter
800g [1¾lb] spinach, well rinsed
lemon juice, to taste

Bring a saucepan of water to the boil. Boil the rye for 25–30 minutes, or until tender, then drain. Drain in a colander. Season the monkfish with salt and pepper.

Find 2 frying pans. Heat the oil in the first and sauté the onion, garlic, nutmeg and cooked rye for a few minutes. Melt the butter in the other pan and fry the fish for 2 minutes on each side.

Add the spinach to the pan with the rye and season to taste with lemon juice, salt and pepper. Serve the monkfish, spinach and rye together.

Sanchez

Rosio Sanchez, a former pastry chef at noma (page 97), has opened her own place in **Istedgade**, Vesterbro. It serves everyday Mexican food and it is so exciting to have authentic Mexican cooking in Copenhagen. I grew up thinking tacos only came as a hard shell and were served with minced meat, sour cream, grated cheese, salsa from a jar… and that was that. But Rosio serves a careful selection of items on her menu, along with daily specials that are full of surprises. I have had some especially memorable oyster tacos here: fresh, acidic and spicy all at the same time. The place is a wonderful mixture of local *hygge* with an international vibe.

I always think that, if you grew up in the north as I did, you tend to feel a certain isolation, a sense that you are apart from the bustling world while longing to be in the thick of it. I stand in Copenhagen and look out, southwards, to the world: there is more of it in front of me than there is behind me, and I am *definitely* not in the middle! Sanchez brings us Copenhageners a bit closer to the beating heart. (See page 166 for Hija de Sanchez.)

Noodle House

One of my favourite places in Vesterbro is Noodle House in **Abel Cathrines Gade**. It is close to not being a restaurant with only four tables. The service is casual, but it's the best Chinese food in town, and it is authentic with a wide range of dishes, and beer served in bottles. It is my husband's all-time favourite place to eat.

Sort Kaffe & Vinyl

Black Coffee & Vinyl – the name of the place says it all. They are passionate about vinyl and coffee, and lots of locals hang out here. It doesn't get more local than this.

Across the street you'll find **Sicilian Is**, a great ice-cream place with organic Sicilian ice cream and a range of Nordic flavours, such as sea buckthorn.

Cafe Dyrehaven

On **Sønder Boulevard**, you'll find an old pub that has been transformed into a café. It's worth a visit, as it is fun and busy with good food. The first time I was there, it reminded me of gastropubs in the UK. They have a great breakfast menu and also serve simple-but-great *smørrebrød* on rye bread. They are famous both for their potato salad and their chicken salad on rye bread.

Pizzeria 54

This is a real casual place. They serve thin-crust pizza and, I believe, the world biggest spritz. In summer you can sit outside.

Right and opposite: Sanchez

Potato on rye smørrebrød

Serves 4

4 slices of rye bread (see page 264 for homemade)
4 tsp salted butter
12 cold boiled waxy salad potatoes, such as Charlotte
4 Tbsp mayonnaise (see page 56 for homemade)
4 Tbsp finely chopped red onion
4 Tbsp cress
4 Tbsp Fried onions (see below)
sea salt and freshly ground black pepper

Place the rye bread slices on a chopping board and spread the butter evenly on each slice. Slice the potatoes and place them on the bread. Place 1 Tbsp of the mayonnaise on each in the middle. Next to the mayonnaise place the red onions and cress. Top with the fried onions. Sprinkle it all with salt and pepper and serve.

Fried onions

Makes about 500g [1lb 2oz]

750g [1lb 10oz] onions, finely sliced
50g [2oz] plain [all-purpose] flour
1 Tbsp sea salt, plus more to finish
500ml–1 litre [2–4 cups] flavourless vegetable oil, to deep-fry

Place the sliced onions in a bowl with the flour and salt and mix very well until the onions are coated. Pour them into a sieve [strainer] and shake, to get rid of any excess flour.

Half-fill a deep frying pan with the vegetable oil and set over a medium heat. Make sure the oil is hot by placing a slice of onion in it: if it sizzles, it is ready. Reduce the heat a little and add one-third of the sliced onions. Careful, it may spit! Don't leave the pan; instead, stir occasionally with a slotted spoon. Fry until light brown and crispy.

Using the slotted spoon, transfer the onions to a plate lined with kitchen paper [paper towels] and sprinkle with a little more salt. Repeat the process with the remaining 2 batches of onions.

Kihoskh

My friend and neighbour Keld Pedersen
owns this place on **Sønder Boulevard**. It is
probably one of the world's best corner shops,
with an amazing selection of beers and organic
produce, great magazines, local literature,
good coffee and bread from its own bakery.
You can sit outside, drink coffee and feel part
of the neighbourhood. Keld is a very good
cook and always the grill master when we
are cooking at home in our street (page 237).
Keld's hospitality makes this a real destination
for locals, who flock here to buy bread, pick up
the newspaper or just have a chat before the
day begins. It is a great example of the joy that
living in cities can bring.

Brød

Brød is an organic bakery in **Enghave Plads**.
This is part of Keld's small empire, with a nice
range of bread, Danish pastries and cakes.

Absalons church

This is an old church made into a communal
space, with dinner served at a long table. Arrive
early, as they take no reservations, and it is
strictly first come, first served. The inexpensive
food is presented family style, the atmosphere
is fun and lively and they also host dancing
events, yoga and a lot of other great activities.

Itzi Pitzi Pizza

Next to Kihoskh is small pizzeria owned by
Keld's friend, Klaus. You can buy pizza and eat
it outside in the space Keld has created.

Vesterbro has an arthouse cinema, **Vester
Vov Vov**, which has the smallest screen but
is very *hyggelig* in the true sense of the
word. It always shows a great repertoire
of world and European cinema. Well before
other cinemas figured this out, you could
bring a coffee or a glass of wine into the
screening room.

Opposite: Kihoskh. Above: Brød

Beetroot and salmon sandwiches on rye bread

You can buy rye bread sandwiches all over Copenhagen; rye is very much part of the Danish culture. These days, I find I am seeing rye bread, *smørrebrød* and open sandwiches in more and more places around the world, and that makes me very happy.

Makes 4

For the dressing
4 Tbsp natural [plain] yogurt
4 Tbsp mayonnaise (see page 56 for homemade)
2 Tbsp chopped dill
2 Tbsp chopped chives
1 Tbsp lemon juice
sea salt and freshly ground black pepper

For the sandwiches
8 slices of rye bread (see page 264 for homemade)
4 large lettuce leaves
4 slices of smoked salmon
2 x Beetroot and celeriac cakes (page 209)

Mix all the ingredients for the dressing in a bowl, seasoning to taste with salt and pepper.

For the sandwiches, place the rye bread on a work top. Spread the dressing on the rye bread. Place lettuce leaves on 4 slices of the bread. Top 2 of these with the salmon and the other 2 with the beetroot and celeriac cakes. Place the other 4 slices of rye bread on top. Wrap and serve.

You can use any leftover vegetable patties or falafels for the sandwiches.

Cardamom buns

Cinnamon rolls always used to be the big thing in Copenhagen, but these days it is all about cardamom *snurre*. These are perfect either for breakfast or afternoon tea.

Makes 18–20

For the buns
50g [2oz] fresh yeast
500ml [2 cups] lukewarm
    whole milk
1 egg, lightly beaten
850g [6 cups] '00' flour,
    plus more to dust
100g [½ cup] caster [granulated]
    sugar
2 tsp ground cardamom
½ tsp fine sea salt
150g [⅔ cup] softened salted
    butter

For the filling
200g [¾ cup plus 2 Tbsp]
    softened salted butter
150g [¾ cup] caster [granulated]
    sugar
4 tsp ground cinnamon

For the buns, crumble the yeast into the milk and stir to dissolve, then add the egg. Now mix in the flour, sugar, cardamom and salt. Mix the butter into the dough, then knead well on a floured surface. Put the dough into a bowl, cover with a tea towel and leave to rise in a warm place for 1–2 hours, or until doubled in size.

Make the filling by mixing together the butter, sugar and cinnamon. Divide the dough in half and roll each piece out on a floured surface to make a rectangle measuring about 40 x 30cm [16 x 12in]. Spread half the cinnamon filling over each. Roll each piece of dough into a wide cylinder, starting from a long side to get a long, slim log, then cut into 2.5cm [1in] slices. If you're feeling adventurous, you can then stretch and twist the slices into elaborate shapes.

Line some baking sheets with baking parchment. Place the cinnamon rolls on the parchment, pressing down on each so that they spread slightly. Cover with tea towels and leave to rise again, in a warm place, for 30 minutes.

Preheat the oven to 180°C/350°F/Gas 4. Bake the cinnamon buns for 25–30 minutes until well browned. Leave to cool on a wire rack before serving.

Tivoli Gardens

Many cities have theme parks; few have them permanently placed right in the middle of the city centre. But then, Tivoli is more than a theme park. It has a great music programme, plus it is home to a wide selection of restaurants, some of them very good.

As a child, I had an annual subscription to Tivoli Gardens. After school, my friends and I would go there, not to spend any money (we didn't have any), but to play in the big playground, look at the flowers, listen to the Tivoli guards play music on their daily marching drills and watch the pantomime. These are still among a surprising number of things you can do without money at the gardens (though you do need to pay an entrance fee), and if you bring your own lunch, it is an economical way to spend a day.

I worked as a waitress in the restaurant pictured here at Tivoli Gardens in the 1980s. I learned a lot from the old-school waitresses, who could tell you all the gossip from years ago... though I have forgotten all their stories now. Since then, the restaurants have changed, along with those waitresses. But one thing that remains is the fireworks; they are very impressive, so make sure you see the display.

You will find more than one place to eat cake. Make sure to try the famous Tivoli cake, created by pastry chef Erik Sørensen.

Gemyse is one of Tivoli's new restaurants, with a vegetable-only menu that always leads you on a tour through the vegetables in season. It is lovely to sit here, in a conservatory-style room that mimics a greenhouse. The menu celebrates locally produced food and is also very *hyggelig*, as it is all served family style.

Opposite and above: Gemyse

Waffles with whipped cream and strawberry jam

You will find these in ice-cream shops and street-food carts, but they belong to Tivoli if you ask me. I have always made them in summer, at my beach house.

Makes 12

For the strawberry jam
1kg [2¼lb] strawberries
500g [2½ cups] granulated sugar
1 vanilla pod [bean], halved
    lengthways

For the waffles
1 vanilla pod [bean]
300g [2¼ cups] plain [all-purpose]
    flour
2 tsp baking powder
1 Tbsp finely grated unwaxed
    lemon zest
½ tsp freshly grated nutmeg
3 Tbsp caster [granulated] sugar
1 tsp fine sea salt
4 medium eggs
500ml [2 cups] buttermilk
100g [7 Tbsp] salted butter,
    melted, plus more to cook
250ml [1 cup] double cream,
    whipped, to serve

For the strawberry jam, rinse and hull the berries. Place them in a saucepan with the sugar and vanilla pod and slowly bring to the boil. Reduce the heat and simmer until thickened, stirring frequently so that the jam doesn't stick to the saucepan.

Remove the vanilla pod, pour the jam into sterilized jars (page 56) and seal. Stored in a cold place, this will keep for months.

For the waffles, split the vanilla pod in half lengthways and scrape out the seeds using the tip of a knife. Mix together the flour, baking powder, lemon zest, vanilla seeds, nutmeg, sugar and salt in a mixing bowl. Whisk in the eggs and buttermilk using an electric mixer, then fold in the melted butter.

Heat up a cast-iron waffle mould, if cooking on gas, or an electric waffle iron. Add a little butter, then pour in the batter and cook. If using a cast-iron waffle mould, turn it once, and cook until the waffle inside is crisp. If using an electric waffle iron, just pour in the batter and cook until the waffle is crisp. Repeat with the remaining batter.

Serve with the strawberry jam and whipped cream.

Beetroot and celeriac cakes with potato wedges

Eating 'green' can be many things; you don't have to mirror the classic potato + meat + sauce formula. This is one of the vegetable dishes I grew up with. Restaurant Gemyse (page 205) is a great place to try new, exciting and delicious vegetable dishes, celebrating just how tasty vegetables can be.

Serves 4

For the beetroot and celeriac cakes

200g [7oz] beetroot [beet], peeled and shredded or coarsely grated

200g [7oz] celeriac [celery root], peeled and shredded or coarsely grated

1 small onion, coarsely grated

4 Tbsp plain [all-purpose] flour

2 Tbsp breadcrumbs

1 tsp coriander seeds, crushed

1 tsp cumin seeds, crushed

2 medium eggs, lightly beaten

sea salt and freshly ground black pepper

2 Tbsp salted butter

1 Tbsp olive oil

For the potato wedges

6 large potatoes

4 thyme sprigs

4 Tbsp olive oil

For the creamed spinach

1kg [2¼lb] spinach

2 Tbsp salted butter

1 garlic clove, finely chopped

100ml [⅓ cup] double [heavy] cream

½ tsp freshly grated nutmeg

For the beetroot and celeriac cakes, in a large bowl, mix together the beetroot, celeriac, onion, flour, breadcrumbs and spices. Mix in the eggs in, then season well with salt and pepper. Leave to rest.

Preheat the oven to 180°C/350°F/Gas 4. For the potato wedges, cut the potatoes into wedges and place in an ovenproof dish. Mix in the thyme, olive oil, salt and pepper, then bake for 30 minutes.

For the cakes again, melt the butter and olive oil together in a large frying pan. Form oval balls of the beetroot mixture with a spoon and a hand and fry for about 10 minutes, turning regularly. Just before serving, make the creamed spinach.

Rinse the spinach well in cold water while you melt the butter in a large saucepan. Add the drained spinach and garlic, cover and cook just until the spinach wilts. Add the cream and nutmeg, mix well and cook for 2 minutes, then season to taste with salt and pepper.

Serve the cakes with the potato wedges and the creamed spinach on the side.

Fried chicory salad

I love the fact that more and more restaurants like to work with vegetables, getting far more interesting dishes from them than used to be the case, and sticking more strictly to seasonality.

Serves 4

200g [7oz] beetroot [beet]
2–3 Tbsp balsamic vinegar
2 heads of white chicory [endive]
1 head of red chicory [endive]
2 shallots
1 Tbsp salted butter
5 wild garlic leaves or chives, sliced
1 Tbsp extra virgin olive oil
2 Tbsp lemon juice
sea salt and freshly ground black pepper

Preheat the oven to 110°C/225°F/Gas ¼.

Bring a saucepan of lightly salted water to the boil. Peel the beetroot and boil for 30 minutes, then drain and cut it into super-thin slices. Place on a baking sheet lined with baking parchment and brush with the balsamic vinegar. Bake for 1 hour.

Quarter each white chicory head lengthways; separate the leaves of the red chicory. Peel and cut the shallots into 3 pieces each. Melt the butter in a frying pan and fry the shallots, cut side down, making sure they caramelize. Remove from the saucepan and set aside.

Fry the white chicory in the butter on all sides. Place on a serving dish with the red chicory leaves, beetroot crisps, shallots and wild garlic leaves or chives.

Whisk together the olive oil and lemon juice and season well with salt and pepper. Drizzle over the salad and serve right away.

Nørrebro

This area is the most diverse in Copenhagen, attracting people of many different cultures from all around the world. Historically, immigrants settled in this district because the housing was affordable in the 1970s and 1980s, and it is now the most populous of all the boroughs in the city. You'll find Indian, Pakistani, Iranian, Turkish, Lebanese and Somali shops, restaurants and coffee houses.

To get to Nørrebro from the city centre, you need to cross **Dronning Louises Bridge**, a great spot in the summer from which to watch the sunset, and sometimes the site for street parties, both official and unofficial!

Nørrebro was run-down in the 1970s and 1980s, and the traditional Danish shops were closing, but that afforded the opportunity for new citizens to move in. A range of exciting shops opened and suddenly you could get aubergines, pomegranates, limes, fresh coriander (I had never tasted it before), more unusual herbs, unknown spices, rosewater and halal meat.

In culinary terms, the 1980s was like a new world: we 'discovered' avocado and kiwi fruit, fresh root ginger and basmati rice, having grown up on American long grain. So many things we take for granted today were brought to Copenhagen by immigrants, who imported them because they were missing their homeland's ingredients.

I shared a five-bedroom apartment with friends here in the late 1980s while I started up a radio station and tried to improve my A-level grades to get into university. As a child, I remember coming here with grown-ups to buy spices, chickpea paste and tahini for hummus, as well as fresh-baked pitta bread. In my late teens and early twenties, a lot of my friends had flats here; they were affordable, and the area was not yet gentrified. You could buy apartments in buildings with shared ownership cheaply and pay a very low rent. Those days are over. The grotty old pubs, which I didn't dare go into as a young woman, have closed down. All the backyards have been cleared to make room for shared gardens and courtyards. And it is not a left wing-only area any more! It is a great place and has never been dangerous; it just erupts from time to time. It also has big council estates, where immigrant families live, some with a lot of social challenges.

Historically, Nørrebro has always been the troubled part of town, a bit of a battlefield, where outsiders have clashed with the establishment. For the last 150 years it has been a real working-class area, with squatters trying to save the old buildings from being torn down. I think few today could argue they were not correct: restoring the buildings was a much better idea than demolishing them and building 1970s housing (which never became anybody's favourite architecture).

Before the mid-19th century, Nørrebro was countryside; you came here to enjoy the fresh air. It was an area of market gardens, renowned for their excellent rhubarb, so people called it the 'rhubarb neighbourhood'. This name clung to a part of the district long after the last rhubarb plant had been cleared.

Aubergine salad with pomegranate

Aubergine was one my favourite foods as a child and I still experiment a lot with them, mixing them with all the lovely things I find in the greengrocers at Nørrebro. I am also inspired by what I learned from the cooking of the Palestinians who were among my parents' friends.

Serves 4

For the salad
2 large aubergines [eggplant]
3 Tbsp olive oil
sea salt and freshly ground
   black pepper
1 pomegranate
1 green chilli
100g [3½oz] feta cheese, crumbled
leaves from a small bunch of mint

For the dressing
1 Tbsp lemon juice
1 Tbsp extra virgin olive oil

Preheat the oven to 180°C/350°F/Gas 4.

For the salad, halve the aubergines lengthways, cut each half into long wedges and then cut into 5cm [2in] pieces. Put them in a bowl and mix with the olive oil, salt and pepper. Place on baking sheet lined with baking parchment. Bake for 20 minutes. Remove from the oven and leave to cool.

While the aubergines cool, halve the pomegranate and take out the arils, and finely slice the chilli.

In a small bowl, whisk the lemon juice and olive oil together to make the dressing.

Place the aubergine on a serving platter with the feta, pomegranate, chilli and mint. Drizzle the dressing over, sprinkle with salt and pepper and serve right away.

Indre Nørrebro

This neighbourhood around **Sankt Hans Square** used to be corner shops, greengrocers and second-hand traders. There were dodgy pubs and no cafés, but there was a nice cafeteria on the corner of Guldbergsgade with neon lights, laminated tables, freshly made filter coffee and sliced white bread with cheese and slivers of green pepper on top. If you went there early in the morning, you'd be with taxi drivers and true locals. Now the whole neighbourhood has a lot of cafés with croissants, sourdough buns and lattes. You would be hard-pushed to find regular white bread!

The change started in the 1990s. **Elmegade** used to be the darkest, dirtiest street you could imagine, where you only went if you needed a cheap second-hand refrigerator as a student, or if you had to bicycle through it to get to the other end of town. Now it has sushi and juice bars, good coffee and edgy fashion stores.

At the corner of Elmegade and Sankt Hans Square is a coffee bar I often visit, **Kaffeplantagen**. Further down **Gulbergsgade** is the **Herslev** beer bar, **Grød** (page 222) and **Kiin Kiin** (a well-known Thai place). The place is teeming with opportunities to have a good time. Without wishing to sound ancient, I am still amazed when I see what Nørrebro is now compared to how it was when I lived here. I would not in my wildest dreams have thought it would be possible. I hope it can stay this way and hold on to its diversity.

Here you will also find **Mirabelle** and **Bæst**, two pioneer restaurants working with sustainable solutions and both part of Christian Puglisi's restaurant group. Christian has played a big role in the transformation of Copenhagen, being also responsible for Relæ and Manfreds. At Mirabelle you can get simple, tasty Italian food, majoring on pasta and vegetables with a little meat. You can also buy great sourdough bread; I often bicycle here at the weekend to pick up freshly baked sourdough or croissants, or take a detour on my morning walks around the lakes. If you prefer, you can sit outside and enjoy a coffee.

Bæst bakes pizza in a wood-fired oven. The pizza bases (using local organic flour) and toppings are all prepared in-house: the salumi and mozzarella are both made on the second floor. You can also buy their fresh mozzarella, created from local milk, which is so creamy and wonderful that you will never again want the gooey pretender you can buy in the supermarket. Treat yourself to a great Nørrebro night out with pizza at Bæst followed by a movie at the **Empire**, an independent cinema, next door. The Empire is my local cinema; they have a good programme of films, comfortable seats and (of course) great places to eat before or after the movie.

Left: Bæst, where they make their own mozzarella

Nordic pizza

You could debate whether this is a pizza or a crispbread with vegetables. I really like the crust: the rye flour gives a nice flavour that works wonderfully well with potatoes and kale. You can buy good pizza in Copenhagen, but there is also a lot of rubbish pizza, so choose with care!

Makes 2 x 35cm [14in] pizzas; serves 4

For the base
25g [1oz] fresh yeast
300ml [1¼ cups] lukewarm water
300g [2½ cups] wholegrain stoneground rye flour, plus more to dust
50g [6 Tbsp] plain [all-purpose] flour
1 tsp fine sea salt
olive oil, to brush

For the topping
600g [1lb 5oz] potatoes, very thinly sliced
200g [7oz] kale leaves, coarse stalks removed, well rinsed, drained and finely chopped
2 red onions, sliced
100g [3½oz] Vesterhavs or Parmesan cheese, grated
4 Tbsp extra virgin olive oil, plus more to brush
½ tsp freshly grated nutmeg
sea salt and freshly ground black pepper

For the base, dissolve the yeast in the water in a big mixing bowl, then add both flours and the salt. Mix to a dough, then knead well on a floured surface until smooth. Cover the bowl with a tea towel and leave to rise for 2 hours at room temperature.

Preheat the oven to 220°C/425°F/Gas 7.

Roll the dough out on a lightly floured surface into 2 very thin circles, then place on a lightly oiled baking sheet.

For the topping, mix together the potato slices, kale, red onions, cheese, extra virgin olive oil, nutmeg, salt and pepper, divide it evenly over the pizza dough, brush again with olive oil and sprinkle with some salt and pepper.

Bake the pizzas for 20–25 minutes until the topping and crust are nicely browned. Brush the edges with extra virgin olive oil as soon as they come out of the oven, then serve.

Jægersborggade

This street is the epitome of gentrification, with its cobblestones, great apartments, coffee shops, restaurants, chocolatiers, ceramics boutiques and even its own **Michelin-star** restaurant. But if you could roll back time, you would see that it used to be dominated by Hell's Angels and small-time drug dealers. It was rough and dirty and people managed to get on with their lives… even without hipster coffee.

I have friends who started businesses here back in the day, when rent was cheap, so creative people with great ideas but no money had a chance to get their foot in the door. I hope this interesting spark, the thing that made Jægersborggade special and accessible, isn't snuffed out. When popularity grows, money follows.

Relæ

This experimental, high-end restaurant was one of the drivers of change in Nørrebro. It opened in Jægersborggade back when drug dealers were still selling right outside the door. It has a gold rating, which means the food is 90–100% organically sourced; that fact is very inspiring, as it is not easy to do in Copenhagen, with its limited range of produce during the cold winter months. I have been lucky enough to enjoy a lot of great meals at Relæ, including the rye porridge 'ollebrød' (page 224) and scorched cabbage in its own juice. It is modern Danish food, made from the best organic ingredients each month has to offer. The thing to remember about seasonality in Copenhagen is that we do not only have four seasons, but more like eight or nine, since things change often and no weather hangs around for too long.

Grød

This is now a chain, though the first site was in Jægersborggade. They serve only porridge, though it's far more delicious and versatile than that might sound. The word 'grød' means 'porridge'. It was always part of Nordic culture. I grew up on porridge; it's cheap and keeps you going.

Many Danish people were brought up with Monday 'porridge night', but it disappeared during the 1980s and by the 1990s – when we were wealthier than ever before – we had forgotten it ever existed; the food scene was all about Thai, Italian or Japanese cuisines. However, in the 2000s, porridge entered the Danish food scene again along with the new Nordic movement, when getting back to our roots became aspirational. Grød opened and millers started to make porridge mix for both breakfast and dinner.

One place I always check out when I am in the neighbourhood is ceramicist **Inge Vincent's workshop**, which has super-delicate feminine pieces. I love her cups and vases and little candle holders.

Right: Jægersborggade. Opposite: Grød

Porridge, four ways

All recipes serve 4

Ollebrød
500g [1lb 2oz] rye bread,
   preferably stale
1 litre [4 cups] water
finely grated zest of 1 and juice
   of $\frac{1}{2}$ unwaxed lemon
100ml [$\frac{1}{3}$ cup] golden [corn] syrup
whipped cream or whole milk,
   to serve

Rice porridge
250ml [1 cup] water
300g [1$\frac{1}{2}$ cups] short-grain
   pudding rice
1.5 litres [6$\frac{1}{2}$ cups] whole milk
1 tsp sea salt
6 Tbsp caster [granulated] sugar
2 Tbsp ground cinnamon
55g [4 Tbsp] chilled salted butter

Apple 'porridge'
2kg [4$\frac{1}{2}$oz] eating apples,
   such as Cox
1 vanilla pod [bean]
2–3 Tbsp water
50–100g [$\frac{1}{4}$–$\frac{1}{2}$ cup] caster
   [granulated] sugar
200ml [$\frac{3}{4}$ cup] double [heavy]
   cream

Fruit 'porridge'
1 vanilla pod [bean]
200g [2 cups] blackcurrants
200g [2 cups] redcurrants
500g [1lb 2oz] strawberries
150–200g [$\frac{3}{4}$–1 cup] caster
   [granulated] sugar, to serve
4 Tbsp water
2 Tbsp cornflour [cornstarch]
chilled single [light] cream or
   whole milk

Ollebrød
The night before, crumble the bread into a bowl, cover with the water and leave overnight. The next day, transfer to a heavy-based pan, slowly bring to the boil, then simmer, whisking, until smooth. Add the lemon juice and simmer, stirring, for 5 minutes, then take off the heat and stir in the zest and syrup. Serve warm with cream or milk, sprinkled with more lemon zest if you like.

Rice porridge
Pour the water into a heavy-based pan and bring to the boil. Add the rice and boil for 2 minutes, stirring. Add the milk and return to the boil, stirring constantly. Cover with a lid, reduce the heat and simmer for 45 minutes, stirring now and then. Remove from the heat and add the salt. Mix the sugar and cinnamon together in a small bowl. Serve the porridge in 4 dishes. Make a dent with a spoon in the middle of each portion and add a spoonful of cold butter. Sprinkle with the cinnamon sugar and serve.

Apple 'porridge'
Core and peel the apples, then cut them into small cubes. Split the vanilla pod in half lengthways. Place the apples and vanilla in a pan with the water and the smaller amount of sugar. Slowly bring to the boil, stirring frequently, then reduce the heat and simmer for 15–20 minutes until it has become a lumpy purée. Sweeten with more sugar, if needed. Pour into 4 small bowls, then leave to cool completely. Before serving, whip the cream. Place 2–3 Tbsp of the cream on top of each bowl. Serve the rest of the cream on the side.

Fruit 'porridge'
Split the vanilla pod in half lengthways. Top and tail the currants; hull and halve the strawberries. Place the fruit in a pan with the vanilla, the smaller amount of sugar and half the water. Bring to the boil, skimming any froth from the top. Reduce the heat and simmer until the currants burst. Sweeten with more sugar, if needed. Mix the cornflour with the remaining 2 Tbsp water. Increase the heat under the fruit and bring to the boil, then little by little stir in the cornflour mixture until thickened. (You may not need it all.) Pour the 'porridge' into bowls, sprinkle with sugar and serve cold with cream or milk.

Assistens Kirkegård

This place is both a public park and a cemetery, and is an important leisure space in this neighbourhood. It has beautiful walkways and areas with both old and new graves. Ordinary Copenhagen citizens are buried here alongside Danish nobility such as **Hans Christian Andersen**, **Niels Bohr** and **Søren Kierkegaard**.

It is a wonderful place to sit and read, to bicycle through, to get lost in the overgrown parts or just to walk around, read the tombstones and think about all these remarkable people. Residents in Nørrebro use it as their park, they have picnics and birthdays parties here or take a break among the tombstones during the day. I think it is a special, unique place. It is magical, especially around twilight when the cemetery starts to get dark but you still have the warm yellow light above you. If I have time, I always get off my bike and walk slowly through.

Østerbro

I was born and lived my first months in Østerbro, not in the posh part, but on Blegdamsvej, a street named after the workshops that bleached cotton here 170 years ago when the area was still out of town. It is also where I live now, though I've lived most of my life in central Copenhagen.

Some would say Østerbro is a slightly dull area for young families. It is nicknamed '2100 Spelt', an ironic postcode reference to the politically correct high-income families who have flocked here with their designer furniture, organic food and preference for spelt over wheat! This is of course a caricature of Østerbro folk, though there is some truth to it and I must admit that my own neighbourhood fits easily into that category.

Østerbro is a quiet district, without as many bars, nightlife or noisy festivals as some other areas. But it is the borough in Copenhagen that is closest to the water: a 10-minute bike ride and you are at the beach and a large marina with its swimming clubs and its sauna for winter bathing.

This neighbourhood has a lot of great food shopping, including health food stores; there is a wonderful fishmonger – **Dagens Fisk** on Østerbrogade – and a **Saturday market** on Sankt Jacobs Plads where you will find **Danial Letz's delicatessen**.

Østerbro has many large apartments with three or four bedrooms. The area also has the most expensive property in the city. The main high street leads directly north, where some of Denmark's most elite areas are dotted along the coastline.

While Copenhagen's other boroughs have been growing and changing, not much has happened in Østerbro… Until now, that is, as many new everyday restaurants have started to pop up, along with wine bars, ice-cream places, bakeries and my own new place, **Hahnemanns Køkken**.

And a whole new area is under construction: Nordhavn, the old commercial harbour, is being transformed into a residential area with great views over to Sweden and The Bridge. Cycle out there and experience this new area. Get a coffee at **Original Coffee** and enjoy the sea view. An old grain silo has been turned into a residential building with a restaurant at the top (called **Restaurant Silo**, of course). They have great modern Danish food and some of the best views over the city.

Opposite: Øster Anlaeg

My neighbourhood

My parents moved to a two-bedroom apartment when I was less than a year old, so my earliest memories are from living at Østerbro. That apartment faced the lakes and I spent a lot of time sitting in the window looking out at the water and the large chestnut trees, following the ducks and swans swimming back and forth. In the month of September, I remember crossing the road, picking up chestnuts and making funny little animals out of them.

Øster Farimagsgade is the main street in this neighbourhood, still very busy and with a range of shops and places to eat. I remember the local butcher always gave me a piece of cold sausage to taste. We had an account at the basement dairy shop and I was a bit afraid of the lady who ran it – I guess because my mother sometimes owed her money. Buying *flødeboller* (page 234) from her is still a vivid memory, as is how she would carve out the butter from a large block in the gram weight you had ordered, and clinking home with the milk that came in glass bottles. Some of my first food memories are from that time. I remember sitting in our small kitchen eating rice porridge with cinnamon and sugar (page 224), or rye bread with salami or raisins on top, my mother sitting with me, absent-minded, smoking cigarettes, waiting for me to finish my food.

Now on Øster Farimagsgade there is a **Sticks 'n' Sushi**, **Hønen & Ægget** and **Aamanns**, the original open sandwich place.

Right and opposite: Kartoffelrækkerne (page 237)

Flødeboller

The classic, which you can buy everywhere, often with marzipan as part of
the base. I do not like that version – I prefer the traditional waffle-like base.
You will need a sugar thermometer to make the marshmallow.

Makes about 20

For the waffle base
1 egg
200ml [¾ cup] buttermilk
25g [2 Tbsp] caster [granulated]
   sugar
75g [½ cup plus 1 Tbsp] plain
   [all-purpose] flour
100g [7 Tbsp] salted butter,
   melted and cooled

For the marshmallow
50ml [3½ Tbsp] water
150g [¾ cup] caster [granulated]
   sugar, plus 1 Tbsp
75g [2½oz] liquid glucose
100g [3½oz] pasteurized egg
   whites

For the coating
200g [7oz] tempered dark
   [bittersweet] chocolate
   (page 21)
desiccated [shredded] coconut,
   to decorate

In a bowl, mix together the egg, buttermilk and
sugar for the waffle base. Add the flour little by little,
whisking all the time, until there are no more lumps,
then stir in the melted butter.

Heat up a cast-iron waffle mould, if cooking on gas, or
an electric waffle iron. Pour in the batter and cook.
If using a cast-iron mould, turn it once. Cook until the
waffles inside are golden brown and crisp. Let them
cool on a wire rack.

Cut the waffles into 20 rounds using a 5cm [2in]-
diameter glass or cookie cutter. (This can be done the
day before, if you want to get ahead.)

Now make the marshmallow. Pour the water into a
saucepan and stir in the 150g [¾ cup] sugar and the
glucose. Place over a medium heat and bring to the
boil, then continue to cook until a sugar thermometer
reads 115°C [239°F].

In a stand mixer, beat the egg whites until stiff, add
the 1 Tbsp sugar and continue to beat for a few
minutes. Trickle in the hot syrup/glucose mixture, while
beating, and continue to beat for about 7 minutes.
Transfer the mixture to a piping bag and pipe it on to
the waffle bases. Set aside at room temperature for
at least 6 hours.

Place the *flødebollerne* on a wire rack and pour over
the tempered chocolate, or hold by the waffle base
and dip the whole cake into the chocolate. Decorate
with desiccated coconut. Allow the chocolate to set
before serving.

Street dinner party with my neighbours

In 2001, I moved back to Østerbro with my family to live in a small townhouse. The area is called Kartoffelrækkerne, which means 'potato rows', because the houses here are constructed in rows similar to the way in which gardeners lay seed potatoes in the soil. The houses were built for working-class families as a way to escape the slums of cramped Copenhagen, but records show that it was not so much the working class who moved in during the 1870s, rather the new lower middle class.

The small streets have a car-free section in the middle for residents, called 'play street'. There are community tables, a doll's house to play in, a sand box and mini goals for football games. It's a shared public space and you can use it as a garden, or set up a marquee for parties. We also have an annual summer party in August, a carnival in February and a Halloween celebration. Some families eat together during the summer several times a week, each with their own cooked food. At Christmas, my husband and a group of neighbours barbecue the ducks and geese for our Christmas dinners on the street's big outdoor grill.

My house centres around the kitchen, which tells the stories of numerous dinners and celebrations, as well as all the cookbooks I have written in the space. I love my kitchen; it is the quintessential *hygge*. I get up every morning, light the candles and put the kettle on for tea. I enjoy my mornings in the kitchen all by myself, watching – from the corner of my eyes – the neighbours getting up to do the same.

One summer evening in late August, we got together with our neighbours to barbecue and eat dinner especially for the street party pictured opposite. One of the best things about the Copenhagen summer is the light nights when it doesn't really become dark before midnight.

The beautiful Danish light

Living in Copenhagen is to live with the light that changes throughout the year and often dramatically during each day. I have slightly translucent curtains in my bedroom, so I can follow the light through the night. The first sign of spring is when dawn breaks at 5 A.M.; you sense the morning light before you see it, in the horizon behind the rooftops, and the blackbirds start their beautiful morning serenade.

In the summer, when it doesn't get pitch black during the night, it is like the light is still lurking in the background and never lets the dark take over. In the winter I enjoy the dark. I get up early, hours before the light arrives, light a candle, make tea and sit quietly waiting for the day to begin. During the winter days I even appreciate the murky sky, the low hanging clouds, the colours on the buildings when the sky has spiralled between multiple shades of grey for days on end. All year I love to watch the sun set over the rooftops; from my street behind the lakes, I watch the sky turn bright pink, then yellow, then the clearest light blue. I observe the light all day and how it changes. It is a constant reminder of time, both passing and present.

Grilled steak

Serves 10

10 big steaks
olive oil
sea salt and freshly ground
    black pepper

Bring the steaks to room temperature. Depending on how you plan to cook the steaks, get a barbecue ready (until the coals glow white-hot), or heat a griddle pan over a high heat.

Brush each steak with olive oil and sprinkle with salt and pepper. Barbecue or griddle for 3–4 minutes on each side, or less, depending on how you like it cooked.

Squash salad with rocket

Serves 8

1 butternut squash, about 1kg
    [2¼lb], peeled and deseeded
5 Tbsp olive oil
sea salt and freshly ground
    black pepper
1–2 lemons
150g [¾ cup] spelt
150g [3 cups] rocket [arugula],
    rinsed
2 Tbsp sumac

Preheat the oven to 200°C/400°F/Gas 6.

Cut the squash into 4 x 2cm [1½ x ¾in] pieces. Place them in a mixing bowl with the olive oil, 1 tsp salt and plenty of pepper and mix well. Spread on a baking sheet lined with baking parchment and roast for 25–30 minutes. Remove from the oven, squeeze over the juice of the lemons, then leave to cool.

Cook the spelt for 20 minutes in plenty of boiling water, drain in a colander and leave to cool.

Tear the rocket into smaller pieces.

Mix the squash, rocket and spelt in a bowl and season with salt and pepper. Place on a serving plate and sprinkle with the sumac.

Tomato salsa

Serves 8

1kg [2¼lb] tomatoes
1 red chilli, chopped
4 spring onions [scallions],
    finely chopped
2 garlic cloves, finely chopped
juice of 2 limes
sea salt and freshly ground
    black pepper
4 Tbsp extra virgin olive oil
4 Tbsp finely chopped coriander
    [cilantro] leaves
4 Tbsp finely chopped flat-leaf
    parsley

Cut the tomatoes into very small cubes, draining them in a sieve [strainer] over a sink if they produce too much liquid.

Mix the tomatoes, chilli, spring onions and garlic in a bowl. Whisk the lime juice in a small bowl with salt and pepper, then whisk in the olive oil. Pour over the tomatoes, mix well and season to taste with salt and pepper. Set aside for about 1 hour before serving.

Transfer the salsa to small bowls and sprinkle with the coriander and parsley.

Green salad with radishes and buttermilk dressing

Serves 8

For the green salad
3 summer lettuces
2 bunches of radishes

For the dressing
150ml [⅔ cup] buttermilk
3 Tbsp lemon juice
½ tsp each sea salt and freshly
    ground black pepper

Remove any discoloured leaves from the lettuces. Separate the leaves and tear each into 2–3 pieces. Rinse in cold water and drain well.

Cut the radishes into very very thin slices lengthways, using a mandolin if you have one.

Whisk all the ingredients for the dressing together gently in a bowl. Just before serving, place the lettuce and radishes in a serving bowl and fold in the dressing.

Summer new potato salad with herbs and flowers

Serves 8

For the salad
2kg [4½lb] new small potatoes,
    such as Jersey Royals, skins on
sea salt and freshly ground
    black pepper
leaves from a bunch of flat-leaf
    parsley, finely chopped
bunch of chives, finely chopped
edible unsprayed flowers, such as
    marigolds, roses, nasturtiums,
    lavender and scented
    geraniums, to serve

For the vinaigrette
3 Tbsp white wine vinegar
2 Tbsp Dijon mustard
1 Tbsp honey
6 Tbsp extra virgin olive oil

For the salad, rinse the potatoes and boil them in lightly salted water until tender but not soft and overcooked. Drain and let them cool a little. Halve them and place in a large bowl with the parsley and chives.

In a small bowl for the vinaigrette, whisk together the vinegar, mustard, honey and salt and pepper, then gradually whisk in the olive oil in a steady stream until the vinaigrette is thickened. Taste for seasoning.

Pour the vinaigrette over the potatoes and mix gently. Before serving, place the potato salad on a large serving plate and sprinkle with edible flowers.

Summer carrots with hazelnuts and capers

Serves 8

1kg [2¼lb] carrots with green tops
75g [½ cup] blanched hazelnuts
150g [⅔ cup] salted butter
sea salt and freshly ground
    black pepper
150g [5½oz] capers, drained
    and rinsed

Wash the carrots and halve lengthways.

Toast the hazelnuts in a dry frying pan for 3–4 minutes, then leave to cool. In the same frying pan, melt one-quarter of the butter and fry one-third of the carrots for 5 minutes, adding salt and pepper. When the carrots are just tender, remove from the pan and keep them warm in a low oven. Repeat with more butter and carrots to cook all the carrots.

Place the warm carrots on a big serving platter, then take the last one-quarter of the butter and fry the capers until they start to open and look like small flowers. Sprinkle them over the carrots with the hazelnuts and any butter left in the pan. Sprinkle with pepper and serve.

Marzipan cake (Kransekage)

The perfect choice when you don't want a big dessert,
just something sweet to go with your coffee.

Serves 10

For the cake
100g [¾ cups] blanched almonds
200g [1 cup] caster [granulated]
    sugar
2 egg whites
500g [1lb 2oz] marzipan, at least
    60% almonds (see page 82 for
    homemade)

For the chocolate
200g [7oz] tempered dark
    [bittersweet] chocolate,
    50–60% cocoa solids (page 21)

For the icing
200g [1¾ cups] icing
    [confectioner's] sugar
2–3 Tbsp boiling water

For the cake, whizz the almonds and sugar together in a food processor until finely ground. Add the egg whites and whizz again until you have a smooth, white mass. Make sure the food processor doesn't get too hot, or the egg whites will start to cook. Coarsely grate the marzipan and blend it into the almond mixture. Transfer the mixture to a bowl, cover tightly with cling film [plastic wrap] and refrigerate for a couple of hours, or overnight if you prefer.

Preheat the oven to 180°C/350°F/Gas 4.

Shape the marzipan mixture into triangular wedges each about 3cm [1¼in] high, then place them on a baking sheet lined with baking parchment. Bake for 12–15 minutes, then leave to cool on a wire rack.

One at the time, dip the bottoms of the pieces in the tempered chocolate and place on a piece of baking parchment to set.

For the icing, put the icing sugar in a bowl and mix in 2 Tbsp the boiling water, adding a drop or 2 more if you need it, but make sure you do not add too much. Place the icing in a small piping bag, then use it to draw a small line on and back over each cake, from one side to the other. Let it set for about 30 minutes.

Øster Anlæg

This is my local park, seemingly wild, and the least well kept of all the parks in Copenhagen. The lake and the hilly areas are part of the old fortifications of the city walls. I find this fact is a way of getting a better grip on the idea of time: over the last 200 years, Copenhagen has been built into another city, but the old parts are all still here if you look for them. Øster Anlæg has the most beautiful and very large rhododendron. In spring, I like to follow how it blossoms, day by day, on my morning walks. The rhododendron sits at the edge of the lake and bows down majestically to the waterlilies. I like to imagine Hans Christian Andersen walking here and getting inspiration for his fairy tale, *Thumbelina*.

At the lakeside is a small terrace where you can sit and enjoy your morning coffee. I truly believe that happiness and the essentials of *hygge* come from all the small things you can do on a daily basis, such as going to the park early, bringing your breakfast cheese sandwich and sitting enjoying the light, the sound of the birds and the smell of morning dew.

To create your own breakfast sandwich, **sigtebrød klapsammen with cheese and butter**, spread 2 tablespoons of salted butter over 8 slices of good-quality white bread. Top 4 of the pieces of bread with a pair of slices of Cheddar cheese, then place the last 4 pieces of bread on top of the cheese.

There are two museums in the Øster Anlæg park. One is the **National Gallery of Denmark** where I ran the restaurant for two years and lost a lot of money, so I am a bit traumatized by that. I have not really visited the museum since, which is a shame because they have some of my favourite Danish painters hanging in there, among an interesting collection, and also put on some good shows. The other museum is **The Hirschsprung Collection**, which has a great collection of Danish artists from the Golden Age to the Skagen painters, all worth seeing. During summer, Øster Anlæg is host to a number of festivals and concerts.

Festivals

Copenhagen is a festival city and we have numerous celebrations of music, food and culture. They are so popular now that they define the city's year as it goes through the seasons.

CPH:DOX is a documentary film festival in March; for 10 days you can view interesting documentaries from around the world, including fascinating events every day with a lot of international guests.

Distortion runs for four days in May and June. Huge street parties and underground nightclub events transform a new Copenhagen neighbourhood every day.

Copenhell is strictly for the heavy metal music fans. It takes place in June.

Copenhagen Jazz Festival is in July and you'll find live jazz music all over the city.

Copenhagen Cooking and Food Festival in August and September celebrates food culture, specifically the booming Copenhagen food scene.

Golden Days, a September fixture, is a more unusual festival. It is concerned with storytelling about Copenhagen, exploring who we Copenhageners are and how we connect with our past and the future.

The lakes

The lakes tie central Copenhagen and all her boroughs together. They are in many ways a reference point for Copenhagen, as the city centre lies between the lakes and the port. The lakes are a public space, much used and loved and always crowded with people on the first day of spring. You can take a walk around them – it's only about 7km – and there is a bicycle lane around them, too. You can feed the ducks and the swans (not the Queen's property here); I'm still not sure it's good for them, but children love to feed them! You can sit and have coffee at many places, it's a popular place for dog walking, and you see people running at all hours.

The natural lakes have been reconstructed from streams into more rectangular shapes. They have for decades been a place for Copenhageners to go for walks, even when the area was considered the countryside outside of the city. There are reports that both Søren Kierkegaard and Hans Christian Andersen walked around them. What were they thinking while they walked? I'd love to know. Famous Danish painters such as Christen Købke and L.A. Ring have painted the lakes, portraying people walking here as part of daily life in the 19th century.

I walk around the lakes in the morning and as often as possible; it is a nice way to start the day. You experience the seasons at first hand. In the winter, you see the city getting into action with the rising sun. In the summer, you walk out into the crisp light and chilly morning air, surrounded by the birds' reassuring chorus.

Original Coffee

Walking around the lakes *always* entails morning coffee, which I get from Original Coffee. Coffee bars in Copenhagen maintain a really high standard and there is a lot of proper good coffee around, as well as the more modern acidic coffee. Original Coffee offers a choice of both and I really appreciate that, because I lean towards the more classic flavour and I like to be able to have that choice without feeling totally outdated! Original Coffee has tables outside, so it couldn't be a more perfect spot to have breakfast, which I indulge in when I have the time.

I once had a lecture from a barista guy about the 'pour-over'. I gave him a lecture back on how it was just filter coffee, which both my great-grandmother and grandmother drank everyday, all their lives. I appreciate good coffee and loathe bad coffee, but let's not forget that it is all just coffee!

> Copenhagen is obsessed with cake and bread. You'll find a lot of fun and different places either to enjoy it immediately or to buy it to take home. In Østerbro, I recommend the **Leckerbaer pastry shop**, which has kind of reinvented Danish butter cookies. They are fun, fancy and different.

Top: The lakes
Bottom left: Original Coffee

Soft-boiled egg with rye bread

This is a classic Danish breakfast you will find in a lot of cafés. We always eat cheese and jam on our bread in the morning, especially a Danish cheese called Danbo, which comes in different textures and strengths. My favourite has caraway seeds.

Serves 4

4 large free-range eggs
20g [1½ Tbsp] salted butter
4 slices of rye bread (see page 264 for homemade)
sea salt and freshly ground black pepper

Place the eggs in a saucepan, cover with cold water and bring to the boil. When boiling, set a timer for 2½ minutes if the eggs have come straight from the refrigerator, or a little less if they were at room temperature.

Spread the butter on the rye bread slices and serve right away with the warm eggs, seasoned with salt and pepper.

Yogurt, plum compote and Danish muesli with rye

Most cafés that are open in the morning will serve yogurt with fruit compote and muesli or granola. Here is my signature muesli recipe with rye bread.

Serves 4

500ml [2 cups] natural [plain] yogurt

For the Danish muesli with rye
300g [3 cups] rolled oats
75g [½ cup] almonds, chopped
30g [2 Tbsp] salted butter
1 tbsp caster [granulated] sugar
150g [5½oz] stale rye bread, crumbled (see page 264 for homemade)
100g [¾ cup] raisins

For the plum compote
500g [1lb 2oz] plums, halved and pitted
75ml [⅓ cup] water
300g [1½ cups] caster [granulated] sugar, plus more to taste

Preheat the oven to 150°C/300°F/Gas 2 and line a baking sheet with baking parchment.

For the Danish muesli with rye, spread the rolled oats out on the lined baking sheet and roast them for 15–20 minutes, then let them cool. Roast the almonds in a dry frying pan for 3–4 minutes, then remove them from the pan and leave them to cool, too.

Melt the butter in a frying pan over a medium heat, add the sugar and stir until dissolved. Add the crumbled rye bread and cook, stirring all the time, until roasted and crisp. Leave to cool.

Mix all the ingredients together well and store in an airtight container for up to 3 weeks.

For the plum compote, place the plums with the water in a heavy-based saucepan. Slowly bring to the boil, then reduce the heat and simmer for 15 minutes until the plums are tender.

Add the sugar and gently stir until it has dissolved. Return to the boil, removing any scum that rises to the surface. Sweeten to taste with more sugar, if you like.

Remove from the heat and pour the compote into an airtight container. It will keep for 3–4 days in the refrigerator.

Take 4 jars or breakfast bowls and layer the plum compote, yogurt and Danish muesli in them to serve.

Østerbro shops and restaurants

In the winter of 2017–18, a rumour reached me that something wonderful had happened: an artisan bakery had open up in Østerbro! People were standing in line to buy bread, cardamom *snurre* and croissants, and sourdough bread was being baked in the afternoon. It was true and the place is called **Juno Bakery**.

There are also interesting ice-cream places to visit, such as **Isoteket** and **Østerberg**, with great-flavoured, locally made ice cream.

A nice local place to eat is **Bopa Plads**. In the summer, I think it is the closest we come to the idea of a small village square such as is common in Italy or France. **Beviamo** at **Nordre Frihavnsgade** has great Italian wines, light shared dishes and pasta. The **Pasteur Vinbar** at **Trianglen Square** also serves great seasonal food and natural wines. **Brasserie Barner** is a French bistro and another nice neighbourhood place.

ØsterGRO

This is an urban farm next door to Hahnemanns Køkken with an extraordinary rooftop restaurant inside a greenhouse. It is magical. You walk up into the sky, then you are led into a vegetable garden with a view over the neighbourhood. You are greeted with a drink and a tour of the garden. Whenever I visit, I feel happy. Tickets for the restaurant are sold online. ØsterGRO is based on the subscriptions of its members, who, in the growing season (May to November) can pick up a bag of vegetables every week. Members take part in growing their own food as community supporters of the project, which also includes hens and bees, so therefore also eggs and honey.

Sankt Kjelds Plads

On a winter's day in 2016, next to a godforsaken roundabout with some sad trees and not a lot going for it, I decided that a former discount supermarket space would be the place to open up my dream project, **Hahnemanns Køkken**: a food shop, bakery, café, restaurant, event space and cookery school. Sometimes, you should be careful what you wish for, because you just might get it.

The roundabout is, at the time of writing, being transformed into a park as part of Copenhagen's new climate area, a grand scheme to turn **Sankt Kjelds Plads** into the green heart of a climate-resilient neighbourhood. It will be an urban space, where nature is permitted to spread, but where traffic still flows in the midst of it.

My dream is to create a space where we can eat and enjoy the best that Denmark has to offer. We have a bakery with bread and cakes baked with local flour sourced from Skærtoft Mølle and Kornby Mølle, and eggs from Hengsholt farm. We make salads and tarts, and cook dinner using fabulous vegetables from Stensbølgaard, beer from Herslev, pork from Hindsholm and charcuterie from Steensgaard. We will have an outdoor restaurant that serves organic food, with produce from local farmers.

At our cookery school, you can learn how to cook, bake and make *smørrebrød*. In the event space, we discuss the joy of cooking and the challenges we face in the world of food. My dream is to create an international house that celebrates the food we eat while we inspire each other to do more to save the planet.

Opposite: Hahnemanns Køkken

COFFEE
ESPRESSO   11/15
CORTADO   25
FLAT WHITE   30
CAPPUCCINO   25/30
LATTE   32/37
AMERICANO   20
FILTER KAFFE   20

TEA

BLACK TEA   25
EARL GREY   25
HERBAL   25
GREEN   25

HOT

HOT CHOCOLATE   35

COLD

JUICE   35

Cauliflower and aubergine salad

Cauliflower was a real favourite of mine long before its recent surge in popularity. When it is in season, I make a lot of cauliflower salads for the shop; they often sell out before anything else.

Serves 4

For the salad
1 aubergine [eggplant]
4 Tbsp olive oil
sea salt and freshly ground
    black pepper
1 small cauliflower (about
    400g/14oz)
chilli flakes, to serve

For the dressing
200ml [¾ cup] natural [plain]
    yogurt (preferably 3% fat)
2–3 Tbsp lemon juice
1 Tbsp dried oregano

Preheat the oven to 200°C/400°F/Gas 6.

For the salad, cut the aubergine into 2cm [¾in] squares and place on a baking sheet lined with baking parchment. Fold in the olive oil and season with salt and pepper. Bake for 20 minutes until golden, then leave to cool.

Mix together all the ingredients for the dressing and season to taste with salt and pepper.

Slice the cauliflower, place on a large platter, then dollop the dressing evenly over it. Arrange the aubergine on top, then sprinkle with chilli flakes to taste. Serve right away.

Spinach salad with horseradish dressing

Both winter or baby leaf spinach will work for this salad, which makes the perfect accompaniment to any kind of leftover meat or poultry, or even to smoked salmon.

Serves 4

For the salad
200g [3½ cups] spinach
50g [½ cup] walnuts
2 Cox or other tart eating apples, cored and sliced

For the dressing
100ml [⅓ cup] Greek yogurt
2–3 Tbsp freshly grated horseradish
1 tsp caster [granulated] sugar
1–2 Tbsp lime juice
sea salt and freshly ground black pepper

For the salad, rinse the spinach well in water until clean. Drain in a colander.

Toast the walnuts in a dry pan, stirring until you can smell a toasted aroma and they turn a shade darker, then roughly chop them.

For the dressing, mix together all the ingredients and season to taste with salt and pepper.

Mix the spinach, walnuts and apples together in a bowl and, just before serving, fold in the dressing.

Rye
bread

My classic rye bread. I eat it for breakfast and lunch, and use any leftovers for cakes, croûtons or a crispy crumble to sprinkle over vegetable dishes or salads.

Makes 1 large loaf

For the rye sourdough starter
300ml [1¼ cups] buttermilk
300g [2½ cups] wholegrain
   stoneground rye flour

Day 1
sourdough starter from above
850ml [3½ cups] lukewarm water
15g [½ oz] fine sea salt
750g [6¼ cups] wholegrain
   stoneground rye flour

Day 2
500g [1lb 2oz] cracked rye
250ml [1 cup] cold water
a little flavourless vegetable oil,
   for the tin

For the rye sourdough starter, mix the buttermilk and rye flour well in a bowl, cover with a tea towel and leave at room temperature for 3 days, ideally at 23–25°C (73–77°F). It is important that it doesn't develop mould, but it should start bubbling.

Day 1

If you're making your first loaf from the starter, dissolve all the starter in the lukewarm water in a large mixing bowl (for subsequent loaves use just 3 Tbsp of the starter; see Day 2, below). Stir in the salt and rye flour, cover the bowl with a tea towel and leave at room temperature for 12–24 hours.

Day 2

Add the cracked rye and cold water to the dough and stir with a wooden spoon until smooth (it will be too runny to knead). Remove 3 Tbsp of the mixture to an airtight container and refrigerate; this will become your sourdough starter for the next loaf you make. It will not need taking care of, but it will need to rest for at least 3 days before you use it again. It will last up to 8 weeks.

Lightly oil a large loaf tin, about 30 x 10cm [12 x 4in], and 10cm [4in] deep. Pour in the dough, cover with a damp tea towel and leave to rise at room temperature for 3–6 hours, or until the dough has almost reached the top of the tin.

When ready to bake, preheat the oven to 180°C/ 350°F/Gas 4. Bake the loaf for 1 hour 45 minutes, then immediately turn the loaf out of the tin on to a wire rack to cool. This is great to eat just out of the oven, though it is difficult to cut, so wait until the next day... if you can!

Wheat rolls

These rolls are really easy to make, and the dough more or less takes care of itself. Great for breakfast or lunch, we bake them in our bakery at Østerbro where they are super popular. Danes love bread, cheese and jam in the morning.

Makes 14

10g [⅓oz] fresh yeast
700ml [3 cups] cold water
400g [2¾ cups] plain [all-purpose] flour
350g [2⅔ cups] wholegrain stoneground flour
50g [½ cup] oat flakes
1 tsp sea salt

Day 1

Dissolve the yeast in the water in a bowl, add both flours, the oat flakes and the salt. Knead well for about 10 minutes, then cover and refrigerate overnight.

Day 2

Preheat the oven to 230°C/450°F/Gas 8.

Place the dough on a floured work surface and knead lightly. Form into 14 rolls and place on a baking sheet lined with baking parchment. Spray some cold water in the oven to create steam, then bake the rolls for 10 minutes.

Now turn down the oven temperature to 200°C/400°F/Gas 6 and bake for another 10–15 minutes. Leave to cool on a wire rack before eating.

Choux pastry with rhubarb

Choux pastry is just a winner, and in springtime, I think most cakes should be made with rhubarb. In my world there is no such thing as too much rhubarb!

Serves 6

icing [confectioner's] sugar, to dust

For the choux pastry
100g [7 Tbsp] unsalted butter, plus more for the baking sheet
200ml [¾ cup] cold water
100g [¾ cup] plain [all-purpose] flour
½ tsp caster [granulated] sugar
pinch of fine sea salt
3 medium eggs, lightly beaten

For the rhubarb cream
400g [14oz] rhubarb, cut into 1cm [⅜in] pieces
150g [¾ cup] caster [granulated] sugar
1 vanilla pod [bean], halved lengthways
250ml [1 cup] whipping cream

For the choux pastry, put the butter in a saucepan with the water and let the butter melt over a gentle heat. Now increase the heat and bring to the boil. Meanwhile, sift the flour, sugar and salt into a bowl. Reduce the heat under the saucepan, add the flour mixture and beat with a wooden spoon until a firm, smooth paste is formed and it comes away from the sides of the pan and forms a ball. Remove from the heat and leave to cool for 10 minutes.

Preheat the oven to 200°C/400°F/Gas 6.

Add the eggs to the dough a little at a time, beating well after each addition, until the mixture is smooth and glossy. You may not need all the egg.

Place the dough in a piping bag fitted with a large star nozzle. Line 2 baking sheets with baking parchment and butter them lightly. Pipe a large, thick ring of dough on each sheet – about 30cm [12in] in diameter.

Bake for 35–40 minutes; do not open the oven door for the first 20 minutes of cooking or the pastry might not rise. Remove from the oven and leave to cool on a wire rack.

Meanwhile, make the rhubarb cream. Place the rhubarb, sugar and vanilla pod in a saucepan. Bring to the boil, then reduce the heat and simmer for 6–7 minutes, or until the rhubarb is tender. Place gently in a sieve [strainer], remove the vanilla pod and leave to drain and cool down.

Whip the cream until just forming stiff peaks. Gently fold the cream into the cold rhubarb. Spread the mixture over one choux ring and top with the other choux ring. Dust with icing sugar and serve immediately.

Dream cakes

A classic Danish cake that you find in a lot of bakeries around Copenhagen. It is a pound cake with a sweet and buttery coconut topping that wins people over. I think the home-baked variety is much better than any bought ones.

Makes 12

For the cakes
50g [3½ Tbsp] salted butter, plus more for the tins
4 large eggs, lightly beaten
250g [1¼ cups] caster [granulated] sugar
200g [1½ cups] plain [all-purpose] flour
2 tsp baking powder
100ml [⅓ cup] whole milk

For the topping
100g [7 Tbsp] salted butter
150g [2 cups] desiccated [shredded] coconut
225g [1 cup plus 2 Tbsp] soft brown sugar
50ml [3½ Tbsp] single [light] cream

You will need 12 round tins about 7.5cm [3in] in diameter and about 5cm [2in] tall (e.g. large muffin tins). Preheat the oven to 200°C/400°F/Gas 6. Butter the tins carefully and line the bases with baking parchment.

For the cakes, melt the butter and leave to cool until lukewarm. Beat the eggs and sugar together with an electric mixer until pale and fluffy. Sift in the flour and baking powder and fold into the batter, then gently fold in the cooled butter and the milk. Pour the batter into the prepared tins, to 2cm [¾in] from the top. Place the tins on a baking sheet and bake for 12 minutes.

Meanwhile, put all the ingredients for the topping into a small saucepan and let them melt together over a low heat, stirring to make sure the sugar dissolves. Turn off the heat.

Remove the cakes from the oven and spoon the topping over them. Bake for a further 8–10 minutes, or until a skewer comes out clean when inserted in the centre of a cake.

Remove the cakes from the tins when cool enough to handle and then leave them on a wire rack to cool completely.

Blackcurrant snitter

Snitter with raspberry is a classic in Copenhagen and can be found everywhere. Here is my Hahnemanns Køkken's alternative, using blackcurrants instead.

Makes about 20

For the jam
300g [10½oz] blackcurrants
100g [½ cup] caster sugar

For the base
200g [1½ cups] plain [all-purpose] flour, plus more to dust
50g [heaping ⅓ cup] icing [confectioner's] sugar
100g [7 Tbsp] chilled salted butter, chopped
½ egg, lightly beaten

For the icing
100g [¾ cup] icing [confectioner's] sugar
2 Tbsp blackcurrant juice
freeze-dried blackberries, to serve

Start by making the jam. Place the blackcurrants in a small, heavy-based saucepan and bring to the boil, stirring all the time. Now add the sugar and let the jam simmer for 20 minutes. Leave to cool down. It should be very thick.

For the base, sift the flour and icing sugar into a mixing bowl and rub in the butter with your fingertips until the mixture resembles crumbs. Add the egg and stir until the pastry comes together in a ball. Wrap in clingfilm [plastic wrap] and rest in the refrigerator for 30 minutes.

Preheat the oven to 180°C/350°F/Gas 4.

Roll the dough out on a floured surface to 40 x 22cm [16 x 9in], then cut into pieces, each 6cm [2¼in] long and 2.5cm [1in] wide. Place on a baking sheet lined with baking parchment and bake for 20 minutes. Leave to cool on a wire rack.

Place half the pastry pieces on a sheet of baking parchment. For the icing, whisk the icing sugar and blackcurrant juice together until smooth, then spoon over the prepared pastry pieces. Leave to set for 20 minutes.

Place the remaining pastry rectangles on a board and spread with the blackcurrant jam. Then add the iced tops and decorate each with a blackberry.

Little 'log' cakes (Træstammer)

Yes, this is a cake made from leftovers, but it's a really good one.
Ask any Dane and they will tell you about their favorite *træstamme*.

Makes 10

300g [10½oz] stale cake, such as
    sponge or Danish pastries
100ml [⅓ cup] orange juice
2 Tbsp blackcurrant jam
3 Tbsp cocoa powder
1 Tbsp rum or port wine
200g [7oz] marzipan, at least
    60% almonds (see page 82 for
    homemade)
100g [3½oz] good-quality dark
    [bittersweet] chocolate,
    tempered (page 21)

Cut the stale cake into small cubes. Place in a mixing bowl and add all the other ingredients except the marzipan and chocolate. Mix with an electric mixer into a thick, even paste. Roll out on a surface into long sausage shapes, each 3cm [1¼in] in diameter.

Roll out the marzipan to 2mm [⅛in] thick, and wide and long enough so that you can wrap it around the log-shaped cakes. Roll the marzipan around each to cover the whole log. Leave to rest in refrigerator for about 1 hour.

Take out and cut each log into 3cm [1¼in] long pieces. Dip each end in the tempered chocolate. Place on a tray lined with baking parchment and leave until the chocolate has set.

Outside
Copenhagen

Dyrehaven

If you jump on a local train heading north out of the city, in less than 20 minutes you will be outside Copenhagen. Alight at Klampenborg station. Now you can either turn right and walk to the beach, or turn left and enter the big wooded park, **Dyrehaven**. I go to Dyrehaven at weekends to exercise, but also to relax and to think. Depending on the time of year, I like to bring a picnic, or hot soup, then find a nice spot to sit and watch the seasons change with the light and the hour.

If you choose the left-hand path to Dyrehaven, I recommend you walk to the **Eremitage Palace**, on top of a hill. A big open field surrounds the palace, so you can enjoy the lovely view over the park and down to the sea. On a clear day you can even see across to Sweden. I call this my 'Karen Blixen view' because, somehow, I imagine that it is similar (at least in spirit) to the one she had over the savannah in her Africa. If you find yourself likewise inspired, it would be useful for you to know that the Karen Blixen museum is located a bit further up the coast.

The Eremitage Palace was built by Christian IV to be used for hunting, though it was also rumoured that the king used it to host his mistresses. The Danish royal family still uses it today for hunting parties. The yearly Hubertus hunt nearby each November draws big crowds and is a real spectacle.

There's a large deer population in Dyrehaven, and in the park you can observe them right up close. It's an amazing sight when they start moving in their big herds over the open landscape. It is also fascinating just to stop and watch them when they are in small groups. I will admit, though, when the bigger males come too close, I hold my breath and stand completely still!

I love to walk down to the other side of the Dyrehaven woods to a small village called **Rådvad**, which is very romantic and *hyggelig*. The famous silversmith Georg Jensen was born here. There is a small inn that is open in the summer where you can sit and have lunch on the terrace. In the woods behind the **Rådvad Inn**, I go foraging for mushrooms in the autumn and wild garlic in the spring.

Ordrupgård Museum and the Louisiana Museum of Modern Art

Both of these venues are located outside Copenhagen city, but both are really worth a visit and can be reached by public transport. Ordrupgård has a permanent collection of Hammershøi pictures (my favourite Danish painter), as well as constantly changing shows of both Danish and international art and a famous building designed by Zaha Hadid. Louisiana is located beautifully by the sea, with a view across to Sweden, and is open in the evenings. I go there as often as possible to see the exhibitions, enjoy the view, go for a walk in the park and have dinner.

Right and opposite: Dyrehaven and Eremitage Palace

Carrot, ginger and lime soup with spelt bread

In the early autumn, when I go for walks in the woods, I like to take this soup with me in a Thermos flask, along with homemade bread. It makes a lovely picnic, and somehow the already-delicious flavours are heightened when you are eating it surrounded by all the amazing colours of the woods… and it keeps you warm at the same time! You will need to start the bread the day before you want to eat it.

Makes 2 small loaves; serves 4

For the spelt bread
700ml [3 cups] cold water
10g [⅓oz] fresh yeast
350g [3 cups] white stoneground
  spelt flour, plus more to dust
400g [3 cups] plain flour
200g [2 cups] spelt flakes
1 Tbsp fine sea salt

For the soup
3 Tbsp grapeseed or other
  flavourless vegetable oil
1kg [2¼lb] carrots, chopped
50g [2oz] fresh root ginger,
  peeled and chopped
1 red chilli, chopped, deseeded
  if you like
2 garlic cloves, chopped
1.5 litres [6½ cups] vegetable stock
100ml [⅓ cup] coconut milk
juice of 1–2 limes
sea salt and freshly ground
  black pepper

For the spelt bread, mix the water and yeast in a large bowl, add both types of flour and the spelt flakes and mix well until the dough comes away from the sides of the bowl in a ball. Add the salt and mix again. Leave to rest in the refrigerator overnight.

The next day, preheat the oven to 220°C/425°F/Gas 7.

Knead the dough on a floured surface, then divide it in half. Form each piece into an oval loaf, then place each loaf on a baking sheet lined with baking parchment.

Bake for 30–35 minutes, then leave to cool.

For the soup, heat the oil in a large saucepan over a medium-low heat and sauté the carrots, ginger and chilli for about 10 minutes, without colouring.

Pour in the vegetable stock, increase the heat and let the soup boil for 10 minutes. Now add the coconut milk and return to the boil. Turn the heat off and blend into a smooth soup, seasoning to taste with lime juice, salt and pepper.

Beaches

If you want to go to the beach more than to the woods, there are several options north of Copenhagen. The first is **Svanemøllen**, which is only about 15 minutes by bike from my house, so I like to go there after work to swim. For me, this is a real luxury and one of the benefits that comes from Copenhagen not being too big. Further north up the coast is **Hellerup** beach, and beyond that **Charlottenlund** beach. On this last beach, there's a very well-known club for members only, with an old wooden bathhouse that rests on a jetty constructed on poles in the water, and with a long waiting list. Many people like to swim all year round, so in the winter they will sometimes need to chip a hole in the iced-over sea, and afterwards sit in the sauna! Further up north, in Klampenborg, there's **Bellevue** beach, which is big, and more beaches are dotted along the coastline.

There are beach options south of the city, too. From Copenhagen, you can bicycle to **Amager** beach in 30 minutes, or take the metro. From Amager beach you can enjoy the view of the famous **Øresund Bridge** to Sweden. It's a nice, wide, rather large sandy stretch with lots of beach life going on as soon as the sun is out, and you'll find interestingly designed bathing areas. You have to bring your own towels and camping chairs, as there are no chairs or parasols to rent. But you can buy an ice cream and a coffee.

Opposite: Svanemøllen Marina. Right: Amager beach with the Øresund Bridge in the distance

Index

Note: page numbers in **bold** refer to illustrations.

Acknowledgements

1000 TAK!

Writing a cookbook is a lot of work and without a great team, you can't write a great cookbook.

A special and sincere thanks to commissioning editor Céline Hughes for being a source of tremendous support and understanding. Céline, we did it, and I will never forget how professional and patient you have been during this quite challenging time for me. Thanks to Emily Lapworth for her great design work; and to Sarah Lavelle for her support of my work. Thanks, Lucy Bannell. I love working with you, this time I was really challenged! And thanks to Heather Holden-Brown for love and support and lots of fun. 1000 TAK to the sales and PR teams at Quadrille.

Thanks to my husband Niels Peter Hahnemann for loving me and never growing tired of all my ideas. To my daughter Michala Hahnemann for being there for me and for a clear, honest perspective. To my mother Hanne Rodam for love, support and helping to develop and writing recipes.

To Columbus Leth: thank you for bringing Copenhagen to life, like you have done in this book.

1000 TAK to the whole team at Hahnemanns Køkken 1 and 2. You inspire me every day – thanks for recipe ideas and great cooking every day.

Publishing Director Sarah Lavelle
Commissioning Editor Céline Hughes
Creative Director Helen Lewis
Designer Emily Lapworth
Copy-editor Lucy Bannell
Photographer Columbus Leth
Production Controller Nikolaus Ginelli
Production Director Vincent Smith

Published in 2018 by Quadrille,
an imprint of Hardie Grant Publishing

Quadrille
52–54 Southwark Street
London SE1 1UN
quadrille.com

Cataloguing in Publication Data: a catalogue record for this book is available from the British Library.

Text © Trine Hahnemann 2018
Photography © Columbus Leth 2018
Design © Quadrille 2018

Painting on page 6:
Vilhelm Hammershøi
Interiør: "De fire stuer", 1914
Olie på lærred 85 x 70,5 cm
Ordrupgaard, København
Fotograf: Anders Sune Berg

ISBN 978-1-78713-127-9

Printed in China